The Enigma of Karate Kata and The Corollary of Modern and Post-modern Interpretation

PhD Critical Essay
by Nathan J. Johnson

The Wykeham Press
London & Winchester

Note for the general reader. The term 'Corollary', used in the title, is derived from the Latin *corollarium*, meaning, 'deduction, consequence, inference, [or a] result.'

The Wykeham Press
London & Winchester

Contents

Abstract

Karate kata (formal choreographed training routines) practiced the world over, and long assumed to record and disseminate methods of *unarmed* self defence, are here discussed in light of research which posits key 'antique/ancient' kata (with one, known, notable exception) as 'mnemonic devices', meticulously designed to record, codify and facilitate drills for the use of *specialised weapons*, or more properly, civil arrest tools.

I will contend that these drills (Japanese kata; Chinese hsing) were devised to transmit *specific* weapons skills MINUS THE WEAPONS. I will address the 'why' in the main body of text where I will suggest that these methods were derived from ancient (possibly Ming dynasty) Chinese sources.

There is currently much open debate (on internet forums and through other mediums) regarding the poor 'cage fighting' performances of 'traditionally' trained Karate exponents, including Kung Fu and other stylists who use kata/hsing as a base. These contenders are often easily defeated in modern 'proving' grounds such as the UFC (Ultimate Fight Challenge) and other 'full contact' arenas. I will argue that the 'traditionalist', in order to succeed in these environments, must so utterly adapt his methods, and to such an extent, that it becomes untenable to argue a *direct* correlation between such movements and traditional kata.

This paper also seeks to challenge the dominant position held by the prevalent school of thinking regarding the application of Karate kata, which mistakenly assumes that the kata were designed to be 'creatively interpreted'.

I also intend to address the problematic nature of the reinterpretation of fundamental hsing/kata by Okinawan, Japanese and other students, as effective methods of *unarmed combat*, and illustrate that the corollary of post-modern re-interpretation has created a functionally ersatz art – the thoroughly modern and post modern art of Karate, an art that only received its name in 1936!

Acknowledgements

I would like to take this opportunity to thank past and present staff members of the Students Union at Southampton and Portsmouth universities (and staff members at Oxford, Manchester, Bristol and West Sussex Universities), and those patient university staff members who politely reminded me it was time to 'lock up', when I forgot the time, absorbed as I was with my practice, teaching and research.

Moreover, I have been fortunate enough to have colleagues whose physical abilities in Karate, were only eclipsed by their intelligence. They include:

Sensei(s) **Martin Johnston, Dave Franks, David Blatchford, Roy Smith (MA), Steve Nowaki, Kevin Owen, Kevin Luce, Gary Mcglone, Prof. Andy Cundy, Associate Prof. Dr. Robert Wallis, Dr. Daniel Langton, Dr. Ronnie Ramlogan, Victoria Beardsmore (MA), Dr. Elliot Cohen, Dr. Duncan Thomas, and Dr. Hui Djeung.**

My thanks go also to **Harada Mitsusuke** sensei for inspiring me as a schoolboy, and as a young man, and for instigating my enduring interest in Naihanchi (Tekki) Kata, also to **Men Ken Too** for his friendship, instruction in Korean Martial Arts, and for his exemplary modesty (Meng Ken never wore his obi - belt denoting rank - between the changing room and the dojo).

To **Henri Plee**, who inspired me in both print and through conversation, and to sifu **Kan Wah Chu**t who travelled to teach my friends and I in the late 1970's. My thanks also go to my Kung Fu Si-hing the late **Derek Jones**, and to **'Kam'** (where are you), to sifu's **Simon Lau** and **Samuel Kwok**. Also I thank sifu **Ip Chun** for his gift of exquisite Kwoon calligraphy, and for opening my school, and teaching me at home on the occasions he came to stay. I also acknowledge the input of sifu **Nino Bernardo** and the late sifu **Wong Shun Leung** for their insights into Chi Sao, and my 'hands on' experience with them. Many thanks also go to sensei **Pat McCarthy**, the 'Ivy league', Hoplologist, Karate champion and pioneer, for his input, friendship and plenty more. My thanks also go to **Graham Noble**, an excellent historian, always ready to share material.

I thank **William Cheung** and acknowledge his input through his former resident student **R. J. Gardiner** who taught me during the early 1980's. I thank the late **Yamaguchi Gogen** also through R .J. Gardiner who shared his karate knowledge with me. (He was also a Yamaguchi, Goju Kai Yudansha).

My thanks go to **Rose Li**, (I can still walk the 'single palm change' of Pakua Chang). Thanks are also due to sensei **Mark Bishop** for correcting and 'softening' my Sanchin and Tensho kata during the 1990's, and being kind enough to encourage me with the offer of godan.

My thanks also go to sifu **Carl Coppini** of Bak Mei and Choy Lay Fut, who, although a lifelong contemporary/rival/friend, made me think hard and deep about the nature of unarmed combat - and still does. Carl put senior Kung Fu instructors, an international Kung fu champion, and several well known Karate 'hard men' *on the seats of their pants,* well before such things became fashionable. The only person I know to have beaten him was Eddie Virling. Luckily I never fought Carl.

Thanks to an old friend, sifu **Steve Cox** for coming to do daily 'chi-sau' with me when I was hospitalised in 1979.

Thanks go to sensei **Simon Budden** (godan) ex England Karate team member, Shotokan expert of many years, current Goju expert, friend, and a *first class* Dojo sensei. We have spent much Karate time together over some twenty-five years. Waes thu haele!

I remain grateful to **Eddie Virling** the former 'world class' British ABA ranked light heavyweight boxer who taught me painful lessons about hitting and being hit (concussion I believe), during the six months of intensive coaching he freely gave me. Associating with him sowed the seeds of doubt in my mind regarding the power and efficacy of Kung Fu and Karate.

To my Uechi Karate 'source' who prefers anonymity, but will doubtless read this, I say, your thirty five years of Uechi experience were invaluable to me... Domo Arigato...

Special thanks go the film-maker extraordinaire James Watson, for making a 'silk purse out of a sow's ear'(Ko-do Ryu DVD), I would also like to thank, **Tom Maxwell**, godan, and one of the best of the Kodo-ryu group, (with an excellent grasp of relevant history too). To **Mathew Tasker, who acted as** my patient and physically gifted 'uke' (receiver of 'throws/blows') during the first three years of research. Thanks go to **Mathew Turner,** team member and European Iado champion, also to **James** and **David Faid** (both godan), and sensei **Steve Rowe** - of Shi Kon Budo - who has always acted as a sane, steady and reliable voice in the sometimes crazy world of the Martial Arts. I also thank **Shanir Patel** for his friendship and organisational skills.

To **Marc 'Animal' MacYoung** who not only has my deepest respect, but enjoys a unique, and in my view, *unrivalled* understanding of the nature (and foolishness?) of fighting - Salute!
And to **John Saxon** – Thank you for getting *The Great Karate Myth*

Finally, I am deeply grateful to *all those*, far too numerous to name here, who helped with the arduous and often daunting task of 'restoration', mostly by being willing 'spare pairs' of arms that helped to test-out various hypothesis over some twenty years of unremitting labour.

Note on References and Sources - for examining Professor(s), mentor, and faculty. With respect:
All three publications that contribute to this paper, and my submission, were researched without the use of the internet, although public domain pictures, etc., were supplied to me by internet users. I have however used internet sources in the writing of this paper.

The publications submitted, consist of approximately one quarter of a million words. References, to particulars, events, characters, technical material, page numbers in volumes consulted etc., appear within those publications, but not here. This is to prevent the present paper from being (nothing but) one long list of references and footnotes, particularly as I have set out to write a 'contextualising' paper.

I have therefore chosen to confine *written* sources to those cited in the text. Sources are listed alphabetically in the appendix, and by author and date in the text.

Note on peer review:
Peer review in Karate is problematic. This is due to a number of factors. Of immediate difficulty is the fractious nature of Karate politics, and the fact that there is little formal association with academia. Standards vary too. Moreover, seeking peer review from self interest groups is virtually pointless.

Even the Karate governing bodies (UK) are mostly unsatisfactory and ineffective, and come and go amidst unsavoury allegations.

Rather than relying solely on modern and post modern authors whose publications might lack credibility or authority, or perhaps have a purely populist or commercial slant, I refer you to the endorsements of those *experts* and *senior academics* who are, or have been involved with my research, and support it, this balanced by some public response and reaction to it, (see appendix). As certain kata are, within the body of my work, deemed to be *direct sources* (messages in movement), I referrer the reader to the two seminal books mentioned in the appendix as important sources.

I trust my list of peer reviewers (referees) is acceptable.

Note on photography: All photographs used in this paper are in the public domain.

Notes on the use of terms:
The terms 'Karate' and 'Martial Arts' are written with the first letter in capital throughout, unless another author is being quoted. Okinawan names are written using

the (conventional) family name first, followed by the given name, thus, Miyagi Chojun is used rather than Chojun Miyagi, again, unless another author is being quoted. Use of terms man, he, his, etc. is not intended to privilege men over women, it is merely used to facilitate the recording of material that is, by its very nature rather difficult to record. Man, etc., is therefore used in the best of Anglo Saxon traditions as a non gender-specific term.

All dates used in this paper are current era unless specified by B.C.E (before current era).

I have avoided the suffix 'ka' often appended to Karate (Karate-ka) and used to describe a person, or a group of people who practice Karate. I have used the word practitioner instead. This is simply a matter of personal choice.

I have also generally avoided the term 'bunkai', often used to describe the alleged 'applications' to kata. I have done so because, 'bunkai', along with its commonly perceived translation as 'application', has another connotation of 'analysis', which I suggest may lend undue credibility to 'Creative Interpretation' - discussed in the text.

I have chosen *not* to use the term 'koryu' to describe the ancient kata. I prefer to use 'antique/ancient' instead. I do so to keep the English words uppermost in the minds of readers, and therefore continually reinforce the distinction between antique/ancient kata and modern or post-modern kata.

In this paper, the term *'modern'* refers to kata (and occasionally applications) re-shaped and re-interpreted, for example, by the prominent Okinawan, Itosu Yasutsune (1840 – 1915) and others, such as Miyagi Chojun (1888 – 1953); the time frame being roughly between 1890 and 1936.

The use of 'post-modern' is intended to include contemporary kata and applications as they have arisen. It is also intended to include the standardisation of kata within Japanese (and Okinawan) Karate 'political' bodies such as, the Japan Karate Federation (JKF); the time frame here being from 1936 to the present.

A degree of crossover/flexibility is required in the application of these terms.

The term(s) "antique/ancient kata" used in this paper, refer/s specifically to Uechi Ryu **Sanchin**, **Seisan**, **Sanseriu**; Matsubayashi Ryu **Naihanchi(n)**, and **Kusanku.** Kata such as Chinto and Passai are discussed in my publications but not in this paper. This list remains open to additions.

Also, my work on Miyagi Sanchin and Rokushu (Tensho), both post-modern kata, constitute 'Creative Interpretation' - arguably no better or worse than the interpretations of others. Neither is discussed at any length in this paper.

Without Prejudice:
It is not my intention here, or in any of my publications, to suggest to Karate practitioners that they are categorically 'wrong'. However, I feel it is most important to address major difficulties regarding the application of Karate kata many regard so highly, and to do so in the spirit of enquiry rather than competition.

Thomas Young (1773-1829)

In Memoriam: **Dr. Thomas Young** of Somersetshire, England. Regarding decipherment of the Rosetta Stone; it has been suggested that he conceived (of) an original idea and *Champollion* proved the case - a researcher's nightmare, and the reason why I habitually go into print, as soon as I make a discovery.

Ko-do Ryu
Classical Karate

© Ko-do Ryu Karate and Kobudo 2009

The 'white crane' is a bird whose actions were allegedly studied by the Karate and Kung Fu masters of old. Tradition has it that they imitated the actions of the bird and copied its graceful patterns of movement and defensive abilities. Today, the white crane is incorporated into the logo of Ko-do Ryu Karate and Kobudo.

Introduction

It is my intention here to demonstrate the progression of my published work (three major books over fourteen years) and consolidate their implications and findings in one paper. I consider my published work to constitute an original body of research, aimed at contributing to a better understanding of the *intentions* of the Chinese teachers who created the hsing/kata (formal choreographed training routines) upon which later 'Karate' would be founded.

Karate - often portrayed as a brutal activity - still enjoys considerable international film, television and computer game exposure. Indeed, its presence has become mainstream, which, in itself, whilst not attesting to the efficiency or credibility of Karate, certainly confirms its popularity in terms of its image. Moreover, much of what the layman believes regarding Karate, and its perceived efficiency, is received through these mediums. I therefore recommend that such 'mythologizing' should be taken into consideration during any discussions about, or reflections on Karate.

Chapter One

Creative Interpretation

Throughout this paper, I use the term 'Creative Interpretation' only in respect of applied Karate kata. I do not wish or intend to challenge creative interpretation in other fields.

Popular perception, aided by numerous publications on the subject of Karate kata would have people believe that the *applications* to the kata of Karate, traditionally considered to be the *foundation* upon which Karate rests, have always been the focus of attention for Karate teachers, and the speciality of supposedly combat-seasoned 'masters' of old.

I will contend that this is not the case, and that between the 1890s and the 1920s on Okinawa - the home of Karate - there was a 'paucity of applications', as I discuss in my book, *Barefoot Zen* (Johnson 2000, p. 27). There are many examples I could site here, but one will suffice.

Harada Mitsusuke, Sensei, graded to 5th dan (black belt) by Funakoshi Gichin, the 'father' of Japanese (Shotokan) Karate, told me (Harada, M, *pers. comm.*, 24th March 1992) that:

"*...Funakoshi taught no applications to 'Tekki kata [Naihanchin] at all...*" (Present at this meeting was, Tony Lima and Steve Hope of the Karate Do Shotokai.)

Indeed, 'official' applications are still conspicuous by their absence. A 'thread' on a Martial Arts forum, debating this topic (and there are many, forums and related debates) helps to illustrate my point.

09-16-2002, 08:36 AM	
Sensei Mike ◯ **Banned User** Posts: 44 Casino Cash: $500 Thanks: 0 Thanked 0 Times in 0 Posts	Join Date: Sep 2002 Location: Upstate New York Rep Power: 0

Broken record,

Would anyone like to exchange bunkai for Naihanchi Shodan. I would like to start at the beginning of the kata and include movements for the first direction to the right. I have well over 15 combinations for this kata that I am willing to invest the time to share in.

I would entertain taking it offline via email. In fact, based on the initial feedback on this forum, it would likely be the best medium to correspond. Here, there are several people that have invested some extensive typing time, but not one iota of bunkai has been described, much less hinted at.

(Sensei Mike 2002).

It seems a little strange that the applications to fundamental kata like Naihanchin are absent.

The late Okinawan Karate luminary, Nagamine Shoshin wrote, "...beginners used to learn Naihanchin instead of Pinnan" (1976, p. 148).

Indeed, prior to 1905, Naihanchin were the *fundamental* kata of Okinawan 'Shorin-ryu' Karate. Given that Funakoshi was taught by the prominent Itosu Yasutsune, the enquiring mind could be forgiven for harbouring certain doubts. Did *Itosu* know (the) applications? It certainly seems that Motobu Choki (1870-1944) Okinawa's most celebrated advocate of 'practical Karate' (and a man who based his Karate on Naihanchin solo kata), was forced to develop his own applications. Graham Noble's comments below, regarding Motobu, have important ramifications for my argument:

> At that time karate practice was concentrated on kata. In contrast the study of applying techniques against an opponent in a fight (kumite) had been neglected. As Kenwa Mabuni noted, "A young man taught himself to fight independently - he had no sensei for this". So Choki Motobu was unusual among karate teachers in concentrating on kumite methods. Most of these were his own...

And:

> ...Choki Motobu's books are not very well known, but they do clarify some questions about his karate. For example, it has been suggested that he taught various techniques of Tui-te, the system of joint manipulations and locks that has recently come into fashion. This speculation is not supported by the books; in fact Motobu does not show one locking technique. He always hits... (Noble 1995, pp. 19 - 35)

Yet it is now the case that 'Creative Interpretation' applications for Naihanchin, are appearing - and fast, with many techniques being falsely attributed to Motobu, by inspiration if not by implication.

I am a Karate researcher who does not claim association with Motobu's methods or his approach to kata application! Indeed, I argue that Motobu was one of the first modern 'Creative Interpreters'.

Noticeably, the famous and somewhat maverick Motobu, a contemporary of Funakoshi Gichin, failed to establish a 'ryuha' (style/school).

According to Miyahira Katsuya:

> One reason why he [Motobu] had difficulty in establishing a 'ryuha' was because he was constantly changing training methods. His idea of karate being "living experience" was, in the midst of that inflexible social structure, very un-Japanese-like. In other words, it didn't fit into the Japanese budo paradigm... (McCarthy and McCarthy 2002, p. 35).

I think that *unlike* so many of his contemporaries, Motobu was not happy to concentrate on the performance of solo kata.

Motobu wanted to fight, and did so - frequently. What's more, he looked to kata to provide functional templates. I suggest that in many respects Motobu became the de-facto champion of 'Creative Interpretation' of Karate kata, *and as such, his methods were constantly changing.*

In my view there are two main reasons for this.
1. Motobu's (inherited/cultural) belief in kata as the key to (unarmed) combat.
2. His frustration at the lack of practical applications or explanation for Naihanchin kata. The very kata he considered to be the basis of Karate itself, yet one which he had to constantly interpret/reinterpret.

This suggests to me that the function - the application of Naihanchin - was either, never learned by Itosu, or was not passed-on, as neither Motobu nor Funakoshi seem to have inherited applications – A situation contributing significantly to the current position; that of having a *very exacting*, specific, sequences of solo techniques, but with no clear applications.

Perhaps, the only other options regarding kata passed on by Itosu (excluding Naihanchin) is that they contain 'principles' but no specific applications. I will examine this notion later in the paper.

During the current 'post-pioneer' period - perhaps instigated by Motobu and his reputation for engaging in actual fighting - there is now so much information available on a plethora of fighting techniques from all around the world, and the 'proving grounds' in which to test 'unarmed combat theories', that I suggest, with respect, the subject has advanced considerably from the provincial outlook and limited experience of the early Okinawan Karate teachers and their enigmatic 'inherited' Chinese hsing.

For example, new Karate pioneers like Pat McCarthy, whilst championing the essence of tradition, have taken their (Hoplology) studies as far a-field as Africa. Senseis like McCarthy also have to deal with the global demands that current interest and expectation has placed on Karate.

Personally I do not embrace the modern and post-modern methodology currently used to generate kata 'applications' - modern and post-modern 'Creative Interpretation', particularly in respect of Naihanchin, which is, in my view, a Chinese Ming dynasty two-handed civil arrest/grappling kata, in which the operator remains in a firm upright stance and subdues an opponent, forcing him to the ground, whilst methodically thwarting his every attempt to get up, by means of judiciously applied double wrist/arm locks.

Here is what Pat McCarthy had to say about my Naihanchin theory:

> ...I was fascinated to experience his [Johnson's] theory and application of Naihanchin... If one was to consider it for what it most likely is, a two-man grappling-hands exercise without worrying about politics, uniform, name etc., then I believe that Nathan's theory would be widely recognised. In fact, I bet that if an Okinawan master had come forward and introduced that which Nathan has already done, he'd probably have been hailed from the highest sources (McCarthy 1995, cited by Johnson 2000, p. 177-178).

Ultimately I will assert that *'Creative Interpretation' is the least useful methodology when applied to the antique/ancient kata* in terms of 'application'. Post-modern thinking on kata applications would seem to suggest that there are (potentially) as many 'interpretations' as there are (modern day) practitioners to conceive (of) them. Perhaps that seems logical? Isn't that what a single kata can allegedly teach; adaptable solutions to combat problems? One kata - many applications!

I will contend that modern and post-modern kata *have no 'proper' or authentic unarmed applications*, because they were either created, or developed (in the main), out of weapons kata. And I will argue that the *antique/ancient kata* (except Naihanchin) *are themselves, extant weapons Drills!*

Whilst I do not directly challenge the meanings individual teachers attach to modern and post-modern kata, I question the validity of the methodology used. Finally, I completely reject *unarmed* applications of the kata (Uechi Ryu) Sanchin, Seisan, Sanseriu; (Matsubayashi-ryu) Kusanku, which I describe as 'antique/ancient'.

I suggest that 'Creative Interpretation' is a largely post-modern phenomenon; a method used to glean meaning from kata generally. The quality of 'Creative Interpretation' depends upon the experience, aptitude, skill and imagination of the interpreter.

The general 'rule of thumb' is to make a given application resemble the solo kata technique as closely as possible. This brings its own kind of justification (and kudos) to the interpretation, which in turn reinforces the (justification for) kata.

However, the major stumbling block for 'Creative Interpretation' is that it is seldom able to credibly answer several vital Questions.

For example:

Q. Why is a given kata in the *specific* order that it is in?

Interpreters frequently demonstrate applications to little 'snatches' of kata as confirmation of application. *They are always very selective* – small snippets (often out of sequence) are demonstrated, *seldom the whole kata!* This often gives a greater impression of knowledge than I suspect is held. I am not alone in my scepticism. According to Tommy Pressimone (2008), a fifty-one-year-old Karate enthusiast and ex street-fighter (originally from the Bronx in New York):

> *Practice Kata until the Techniques Become Second Nature?*
> If you read Gichen [Gichin] Funakoshi's early work, "Karate-Jutsu" you will find a couple of examples of kata application. When I say "a couple" I mean that as there are only two or three. They are a little vague and only show a photo and then kind of point in a general direction; like "this can be an application of Naihanchi" or "This is found in Passai." Funakoshi mentions, as do many karate masters of old, that kata must be practiced until the techniques become second nature and can be applied automatically in a given situation. But is this only what they have been told by their teachers, or there [their] teachers teachers? Have they tested this theory? …

What Mr. Pressimone makes plain here is an indicator of the early lack of coherent applications for Karate kata. Particularly as the book he alludes to is *Rentan Goshin Karate Jutsu*, written by Funakoshi Gichin and published Tokyo in 1925 (Funakoshi 1925: 2001).

Rob Redmond, is similarly dismissive, and had this to say:

> …I personally see no evidence that any applications from the past have made their way into our present. I believe that kata application is a wholly modern experience and that nothing was redacted from the original karate training on Okinawa.

> As evidence:

> No published work from the 19th Century or earlier provides applications of the complexity or quality of those seen from instructors today. Historically documented applications seem rather simple.

> I don't remember anyone teaching any complicated kata applications beyond what is seen in Best Karate back in the 1980's. The timing of the rise of kata applications seems tied to the rise of MMA [Mixed Martial Arts] on television.

> It is very unlikely that kata applications seen today are historically accurate to anything done in the past, where [whether?] or not karate practice today exists in a reduction of what it once was… The rise of kata application training is a direct response to the rise of mixed martial arts practice. Karate players [have] been publicly humiliated many times in no-holds-barred competitions, and Karate players are seeking some way to prevent their own practice from losing its market value (Redmond 2007).

Returning to the point admirably made by Mr. Pressimone:

> ...If you read Gichen [Gichen] Funakoshi's early work, "Karate-Jutsu" you will find a couple of examples of kata application. When I say "a couple" I mean that as there are only two or three. They are a little vague and only show a photo and then kind of point in a general direction; like "this can be an application of Naihanchi" or "This is found in Passai...

'Creative Interpretation' enthusiasts sometimes create application routines that *are* seemingly joined together, suggesting they fully explain the kata. But these routines seldom bear sufficient resemblance to the *actual* order of the kata. Even if they do, the experienced interpreter knows only too well, that some segments of his application are more convincing in terms of resemblance to sequence/kata than others, *and some 'applications' would work better if troublesome segments - those bits that just don't feel that effective, or quite match the movement in the kata - could be abandoned in favour of a more direct/practical technique, but one unrelated to the (specific) kata sequence.* For example, an inconveniently placed closed fist dictated by the kata, when for 'your' application, the hand would be better open, etc.

The customary reasoning used to explain these inconveniences is that 'such' doesn't really matter. Kata are mere catalogues. The interpreter doesn't need to be that 'slavishly' meticulous, (despite solo kata traditionally being taught with great attention to detail). The order is unimportant we are told. One can select techniques at random or to suite different purposes. One can reverse the kata; turn it upside down, inside out even. That's the nature of fighting; use what you need, when you want, so long as you win, etc.

Indeed, these are some of the most common generalisations about kata application. I suggest they do more to illustrate and reinforce the problem; *Karate practitioners lack empirical evidence regarding kata function, and the only fallback available to them is 'Creative Interpretation'.* I will offer another example of this confusion in the section titled 'Post Modern Borrowing'. In the meantime I will suggest that the order of a kata is crucial – particularly for primary kata like (Uechi) Sanchin and (Shorin-ryu) Naihanchin.

Unfortunately, the whole idea that proper kata are *regulated military (militia) style drills,* is never considered, because the applications - the purposes - have *not* been passed on, and 'Creative Interpretation' holds sway.

In summary:
Isolated fragments of Oriental kata are re-engineered, to look semi-convincingly like answers to contemporary (pub, street, and nightclub) brawls, set in modern Western urban environments. Context has become seriously compromised; to such an extent that in some quarters, serious *doubts arise regarding both the kata and their applications*. If combat efficiency seems illusive, are the kata at fault, are the applications unrealistic, or *is there a problem with the way kata are perceived and interpreted?*

I maintain that the purpose (the why), and the functions (the how to apply) of the antique/ancient kata, have been lost, not simply because of secrecy (given as the usual reason) or conspiracy, but rather as *a combination of events in history*. A comparison might be to ask: how many 'good and true' Englishmen know how to use a quarterstaff? The only time most people ever *see* one is in a Robin Hood film, (there is, fortunately, a re-enactment revival). I will suggest circumstance that contributed to the loss of hsing/kata functions in Chapter Two, under the heading 'The Weapon Ban(s)'.

Embusen (kata floor pattern or plan) poses another problem for a kata interpreter. It is seldom adequately reflected in application, and often dismissed as a mere conventional formality – something to make kata tidy, transmittable, orderly, or for competition etc.
'Creative Interpretation' enthusiasts explain these and other anomalies by referring to kata as a formal arrangement that will need to be less formal in 'real application'. So informal in fact, that, element of post-modern Karate training have begun to include ground-fighting, which I will consider in the next section.

Is there Ground-fighting in Karate Kata?

One of the currently 'irksome' subjects for kata based combat enthusiasts, is the total lack of ground-fighting techniques in formal kata, given that Karate is ostensibly a combat method, and given that ground-fighting is currently accepted as an element of 'all round combat'. In short (arguably) *Karate kata have no ground-fighting techniques*; they are largely upright affairs. There *are* a few incidences during kata where the practitioner is required to drop to one knee, and there is of course, the famous drop to the floor in Matsubayashi (and other) Kusanku kata, but these could hardly be considered as comprehensive indicators of the presence of ground-fighting techniques.

I offer the following quote, not in retrospective evidence, (i.e. reaching a conclusion and then finding evidence to prove it), but rather to illustrate that *I am not alone in my assertions* regarding the *non-existence* of so called 'Karate ground-fighting' as it pertains to Karate kata application.

The following comments are again from Tommy Pressimone (2008):
> ... I have seen some impressive applications from Westerners, even better than some of the Okinawan stuff at times, it just isn't the same. It isn't the same because it is "their own" stuff. They are techniques that they came up with by studying the kata and using their skill and imagination. They aren't what the originators intended or what has been passed down in most cases. With that said I have to then look at all the ground fighting that has cropped up all of a sudden within traditional training. There have been claims of ground fighting being in kata and that "we have always practiced this." However I think that if a Westerner is practicing ground fighting in class then "he" added it after the MMA craze and Gracie Jiu Jitsu. This is because I never saw Nagamine, or Higaonna, or Chinen or any of the other so called sources of real kata application doing it!

These views indicate, at the very least, that other Karate practitioners are arriving at similar conclusions quite independently. I do not know, nor have I met Mr. Pressimone, but on the subject he discusses above, my views are in agreement with his.

Karate instructors might teach 'arm bars' and related techniques from the ground, but they are not evidenced in Karate kata.

Indeed, such a situation is leading to the creation of 'home-grown'
Hybrid post-modern forms, which, I will indicate, compound the problems already associated with the questionable value of the 'kata' format, in respect of unarmed combat.

Post- modern Borrowing

The Korean art of Taekwondo is a contemporary post-modern Korean style of Karate. It was the brainchild of the late Korean General, Choi Hong Hi, who had previously studied Shotokan Karate in Japan before founding Taekwondo in 1955.

Taekwondo inherited General Choi's modified versions of the kata he had learned in Japan, including Naihanchin (Tekki). So, a re-shaped Naihanchin found its way onto the training syllabus of the post-modern, high-kicking, competitive style of Korean Karate, where its function lay concealed and unknown, and where, in its modified form, it had been re-named Po-Eun, (the pseudonym of the Korean poet Chong Mong-Chu - Koryo dynasty c 1400?).

Notwithstanding this, techniques from traditional kata are seldom (if ever) seen in free-fighting/sparring.

Such a situation raises several questions. However, I will pose just one here. What real benefit does a modified Naihanchin kata provide, in terms of improving the fundamentals of Taekwondo's distinctive high kicking style, it's sparring, or general training, particularly as the grappling purpose of the kata remains unknown?

Common answers to this question might include: leg (stance) training, balance, concentration, focus, speed, power, co-ordination, rhythm, timing, martial spirit, etc. Yet all of these characteristics will be equally well displayed, for example, by a good Muay Thai boxer. Muay Thai is a ferocious art that does not practice forms. So, the Muay Thai boxer would have more time to devote to the art of delivering explosive ballistic power, *unhindered by having to spend significant amounts of time practicing a modified two handed police/militia civil arrest drill from Ming dynasty China*, just to pass a grading.

Indeed, Po-Eun is/was normally a requirement to attain the coveted black belt in Taekwondo, a habit most likely stemming from the styles Shotokan root. Naihanchin, 'Tekki' in Shotokan Karate, was, and in many associations still is, a requirement for black belt status. In my view, the connection is unlikely to be coincidental.

Of course, the onus has to be on me to prove that Naihanchin is a grappling kata. However, supposing for now, and only supposing, that it is; where does that leave the Taekwondo practitioner described above? How many people are really interested in the genesis of the forms they work hard on in the club, and with the people they become 'comrades' with? Most seem to accept a given 'party line' which in this case includes *a history that manages to link a modified Chinese hsing, with a fourteenth/fifteenth century Korean poet who lived perhaps two hundred years before the creation of the kata that (in modified form) bears his name.*

The whole idea of a fluid, free-fighting style practicing rigid - arguably unrelated - patterns is a little odd, and suggests to me attachment to 'tradition' and a slow evolution *from formal Karate to a new Olympic sport.* Perhaps, further down (or up?) the evolutionary road is kickboxing, which often resembles Karate and Taekwondo in sparring, but generally (sensibly in my view) doesn't bother with kata or forms.

I will make two interlinked points here:

First Point:
Po-Eun is arguably, a Korean version of a Japanese version, which in turn is a version of an Okinawan version of the Chinese two-handed grappling sequence – NAIHANCHIN – mentioned above. Answering the question I asked earlier, I suggest that *it is not logical for such to become truly meaningful in* (the context of high kicking – free-fighting) *Taekwondo.* Particularly as I have said, the highly modified Po-Eun pattern is *not* used for grappling.

Second Point:
It is precisely 'Creative Interpretation' that feeds back into the kata, ULTIMATELY CHANGING THE KATA, OR ITS VALUE! Thus, after initially modifying a modification of a modification, (Naihanchin → Tekki → Po-Eun) many Taekwondo schools have *abandoned* Po-Eun pattern completely. I would suggest its relevance was sensibly re-considered.

Here is another example of contemporary views expressed regarding kata adaptation. It is from *Ashihara Karate International* (no date):
> ...Kancho Ashihara had rethought traditional karate kata's... What he has done rather was to modernise karate kata, something he deemed essential to meet the needs of modern street fights...

Kata enthusiasts might bemoan the Muay Thai boxer mentioned earlier, for *not* having kata at his disposal. Indeed, Muay Thai lacks the aesthetics of Karate; there are no weird 'ridge hand' and other strikes (that arguably do as much damage to the user as to the target), there are no 'mule kicks' or 'whip kicks', or aphorisms about keeping a 'still mind' etc., and no 'hidden secrets'. Yet I suggest it is difficult for anyone to denigrate the efficiency of Thai boxers, particularly when they are so successful in violent full contact fights, fights that are far removed from the *choreography* of modern and post-modern Karate kata applications.

'Creative Interpretation' is a retrospective study/addition, meaning that, were Karate practitioners to start the process of kata creation anew, we might see somewhat different looking kata, because the process would probably be as follows:

1. We have a fighting conundrum to solve
2. We must develop techniques (tools) to solve said problem(s)
3. We will record our successful methods for training purposes.

Unfortunately, Karate kata 'Creative Interpretation' goes something like this:

1. I like Karate. It's excellent for many reasons, including self-defence.
2. I have been taught kata. They are handed down from the past. I have been told they form the basis for unparalleled self discovery, combat, and a whole lot more.
3. I think the kata that I have been taught mean XYZ… They need further 'research'. For now, I have gleaned a set of principles.

However, with what can the students of a 'researcher' cross-reference the discovered 'principles'? "Why, with what 'works'!" - is a common answer. But this answer fails to provide an *empirical* or *objective* yardstick. Instead it seeks to coerce the listener into accepting the experience and fighting credentials of the narrator as being true, real, tried and tested; measured, recorded, compared with the encounters of others, observed, verified, etc. In short, the statement says, 'Trust me, I know what works!'

Perhaps, for example, the 'principles' of XYZ kata are suggested as being all about:

'Strength, leverage, lifting, pressing, gripping, twisting, pulling, pushing, percussive speed, ballistic power, hip torque, grounding, rooting, floating, swallowing, vital-point-striking, meridian identification… and so on.

The list can be inexhaustible – and all items are discussed and used to explain 'principles' still with *no authentic method of evidencing* that they confirm the order of the kata or represent the *contextual intention* of the creator(s).

Quite often, such 'principles' state the obvious, (YOU need balance, speed, power, spirit, determination, etc.) and the fact that the 'principles' are largely self-evident, provides a sense of security, security that the 'principles' are right. Progress can then be sought through a continual process of re-configuring said 'principles', creating formulae, and refining emerging 'Creative Interpretation(s)'.

Thus, the observation made earlier by Rob Redmond that applications to kata have become (curiously) more complicated and developed since the 1980s, seems justified.
The principle-based approach can be used to make a kata mean or be *anything the cataloguer, teacher, or practitioner wants it to be*. It is therefore a perfect and primary tool for 'Creative Interpretation'.

I do *not* espouse returning 'all' to a utopian golden age of true, pure or 'real' kata, and I do not wish to be viewed as some kind of zealot or wannabe custodian of 'the true way'. My interest here is academic.

In my view, the *antique/ancient* kata are *redundant* in terms of utility, i.e. as valid and current ways of keeping or restoring civil order using for example the Sai. And in my work I give many reasons why these kata are problematic at best, and highly suspect at worst, in respect of 'all out' unarmed combat.

With respect, I also question the origin and functional efficiency of modern and post-modern kata and their applications, particularly as many of the 'old masters', teachers from a bygone age, avoided fighting. I accept there are apocryphal and anecdotal tales about challenges they received, but few blow by blow accounts exist – records are scant, and not because (as the old excuse goes) the masters were illiterate.[1] Moreover, in the Okinawan culture of the late 1800s, a 'challenge' might constitute anything from a bout of arm wrestling to a contest based on who could perform a kata best!

Those who fail to recognise that I am challenging the 'Creative Interpretation' model rather than (actual) creative interpretations, (process, not result) will understandably feel vexed at what appears to be a most illiberal and authoritarian approach. Particularly if they have investigated and created their own applications to modern and post-modern kata, and found something they believe in.

'Creative Interpretation' of kata is largely an *assumed* post-modern privilege, and a powerful belief system; albeit one that has, in my view, gone 'wide of the mark' in terms of accurately describing and transcribing antique/ancient kata *function*.

It has been suggested, for example, that limiting Naihanchin to only grappling, is to do a disservice to Karate. But I re-iterate; Naihanchin *is* only intended for grappling – that was the whole point of the kata, which I suggest, should be considered contextually.

Yet detractors of my findings will still argue:
"Surely, there is more than one answer to the perennial problems of interpreting kata. There are (read, must be) lots of different answers to kata. Kata have *many layers*, *many applications* for the same physical movement(s)."

But such uncertainty, the lack of clarity, the lack of clear functional directions, (which I suggest was the purpose and construction of the antique/ancient kata) risks the very loss of that which one hopes is being transmitted; and the risk of confusion is high. I sum this up in a hypothetical debate between two Karate practitioners regarding the application of a particular technique in a Karate kata:

"The technique means this…!"
"Are you sure? I think **it** means…that!"
"No, no, **it** *looks* more like…"
"Well, at my last club they used **it** for…"

---

[1] Illiteracy was an unproven charge levelled at Karate exponents of the 1800s, and particularly against Motobu Choki. Far from being illiterate, Funakoshi Gichin - for example - was a schoolteacher and a Confucian scholar. Other influential nineteenth century Karate 'masters', including Itosu, worked variously as clerks, scribes and private secretaries at the Shuri Royal Court.

"WITH RESPECT, I'm a higher grade than you, and my teacher used to live next door to the master's nephew! **IT** CAN BE BOTH!"
"Ok."

The only thing that is clear here is that '**it**' is unclear! Would a 'compos mentis' 'master-kata-creator' risk such confusion, or should we consider kata as a kind of Zen koan, as some commentators have suggested?

A koan is a Zen riddle, originally used to test 'enlightenment', but later, generally used to correct practice. The recipient of the koan is tasked to unravel a seemingly obscure question/topic related to attaining a metaphysical understanding of the nature of existence. (e.g., what is the sound of one hand clapping?) The problem with associating this (strictly Zen) tool, with Karate, is that koan can be, and are, most often, extremely abstract. Combat is not, and I contend, neither were the antique/ancient kata.

Karate practitioners, in trying to translate (access the purpose of kata) erred in the misguided belief that they were dealing with a 'concealed' unarmed art. In failing to interpret such in truly satisfactory ways, they resorted to speculation and eventually mysticism. On applying critical reflection, I recognise that I too had followed that rout in the preparation of *Barefoot Zen*.

Influences upon me included Nagamine Shoshin, who wrote:
Ken Zen Ichijo – 'Karate and Zen are one' (1976, p. 272), and George Mattson (1963, p. 23), who wrote about Zen in Karate, and its (alleged) relationship with Sanchin.

If Karate practitioners are unsure about the *exact* applications (intentions or message of the creator(s) of a given kata), logic dictated three things:
1. The message is garbled (unclear – intentionally or otherwise)
2. WE cannot, or are not, reading the message correctly
3. A combination of both.

The modern and post-modern solution…
'Creative Interpretation', is the modern and post-modern tool, and the norm for creating uses for a host of kata that, it seems, were in the past, seldom given applications at all, let alone specific ones, and this even on Okinawa.

'Creative Interpretation' is so widespread currently as to be almost canonical. *Once the 'Creative Interpretation' 'die was cast', so to speak, once it was assumed that kata were designed to be 'creatively interpreted', the model has ruled, almost unchallenged.*

I suggest this attitude would have been largely unknown in ancient training environments that had neither the time nor the appetite to 'meander' (during twice per week classes, plus seminars) through a 'plethora' of interesting 'possible' applications. Military (and civil arrest) drill(s) must be a functional, 'no nonsense' experience, not a series of experiments. If the (a) drill sergeant has to spend years working out the exotic and intricate nuances of the very drills he is supposed to have learned and mastered during his own training, then something is wrong.

How many prominent Karate (kata application) researchers are teaching anything like that which they were taught? We keep the movements, but we CHANGE THE MEANING. *It is conveniently labelled progress*, yet we remain tied to the kata. How long does the 'venerable' enriching process of mastery take? This suggests to me more of the Confucian values of a bygone age than of a functional art of combat

Let us imagine a golf or tennis enthusiast turning up to enrol for classes...
"How long will it take me to become fully proficient?" the candidate asks.
"Thirty five years or so," the coach replies.
We do not accept such a situation in learning golf or tennis, but we do so with Karate, most likely because Karate is accepted as being mysterious. If one can't become reasonably good at golf in perhaps two or three years, then one might consider changing hobbies.

Child prodigies, spring to mind here. If, for example, you, as an adult, have occasionally flirted with playing the piano, perhaps for ten years or so, isn't it shocking to come across a ten year old giving a virtuoso piano performance?' Your first question might 'How did s/he get so good?'

If Karate mastery really took thirty years plus, then the master exponents might present as quite a rickety old lot. Not much of an army, collectively!

Detractors of this analogy could legitimately claim that Karate is not a military art, but a personal civil art, perhaps of self defence. Despite this misnomer regarding Karate, what kind of practical fighting takes thirty-five years to master? Again, some infer Karate does – It is so deep and so profound, they argue. I suspect that Karate has got that reputation because the kata have been so unfathomable, and there are so many of them.

Post-modern Karate has mysticism on tow, and I do not, as a researcher, apologise for my contribution to that. Research requires the investigation and publication/discussion of all available avenues, and that, for Karate, included Zen Buddhism (by quasi association). Notwithstanding this, it takes - we are told - a lifetime to master the *art* of Karate, but why?

In reality, I suspect that 'Creative Interpretation' is more 'art' than martial, and 'Creative Interpretation' suggests; we have the kata sequences, but they *must* be interpreted, creatively; *not,* it says, because we don't know what they are for, but because the kata were designed that way, because Karate kata are 'multilayered'. It is the belief that the 'old masters' were so clever that they packed multi-layers of cryptic clues into a single kata, and all WE have to do, is work them out. Here is an example:

"By affording a movement multiple applications, great amounts of information could be contained in a kata of a manageable length…" (Abernathy, I., ed., no date).

To which I would add – and great confusion too! The above represents a typical example of the entrenchment of the 'Creative Interpretation' model, (by now I feel want to call it 'syndrome'). *I imagine that, the applications that the author of the above teaches for given kata, are not those taught to him by his Karate teacher(s)*, and, that whilst he may (or may not) maintain an affable relationship with his teacher(s), he does not teach the same (applications) as he was taught; he has 'moved on'. I will warrant he may even feel he has improved on what he was taught, having 'worked hard'. That is why he may have become more prominent than his teacher(s).

But our subject here is not anatomy or biology – it pertains to a number of ancient solo choreographed sequences of 'Martial Arts' techniques (drills) that have clearly lacked definitive explanations, for longer than anyone can remember! *It would seem that Karate takes so long to master because modern and post modern assumptions regarding the function of kata, do not match the kata themselves.* Many Individuals, want the kata to be something they categorically are not, and must therefore labour to create *purpose*.

I surmise that because the square peg NEVER fits a round hole, re-engineering is required. *It is this which always takes time.* Where there is such uncertainty too, many feel (quite rightly) that they can 'have a shot', and do, sometimes leading to the student surpassing the teacher (?) That's normal isn't it? But - of course - depends upon the calibre of the student. Yet as far as the present subject is concerned, misinformation begets misinformation, (the suggested state of Karate kata application).

For example (Stone, 2002):

#11
09-16-2002, 12:57 AM

| Matt Stone ○ **Banned User** Posts: 1,712 Casino Cash: $500 Thanks: 0 Thanked 0 Times in 0 Posts | **1,000 Post Club** Join Date: Dec 2001 Location: Fort Lewis, Washington Age: 39 Rep Power: 0 |

Quote:

Originally posted by Sensei Mike

The ideas I teach are almost all my own, although I do provide attribution for those few in my repertoire that I did not develop myself.

Not to sound like a jerk, but if almost all of your ideas are your own

> (and by "almost all" I would interpret that to mean 75 - 80% or more), what did your teachers teach you? Either you have gone light years beyond what they knew, or they taught you precious little...

I do not undertake here an attack on any individual, but rather the distorted thinking that borrows from mainstream Japanese thought, *and* the educational experiences of the West, to justify its own aims. Allegedly, the students 'kata applications' differ from their teachers, not because kata interpretation is confused, confusing, and becoming increasingly *subjective*, but because of a process known as Shu Ha Ri used by kata-supporting traditionalists. Shu Ha Ri (very) roughly translates as:
Shu - learning stage
Ha - breaking away
Ri - transcending both/all

I might suggest a 'West Point' rifle drill, and rifle range protocols have been worked out very well! Not much need for Shu Ha Ri there. A detractor might suggest that I have stepped outside of cultural parameters – indeed; but, Shu Ha Ri is a *Japanese* concept, not applicable to the antique/ancient hsing/kata from China. The corresponding Chinese three stages of learning are conceptually very different.

'Creative Interpretation' is 'charged' with individuality, which is one reason why I suggest that until recently, modern Western teachers have been prominent in the 'Creative Interpretation' of Karate kata. Their Japanese and Okinawan counterparts are more likely to shy away from such, being affected by cultural norms pertaining to the *collective* rather than the *individual*, and their not wanting to offend the 'master', the 'ryu-ha' (style), and the dojo ('way-hall' - club?). This perhaps can be exemplified through the following Japanese aphorism:
'Deru kugi wah uta-reru' - The protruding nail eventually gets hammered down. Meaning, if you get out of (wah) harmony/line you will be put back in line – hammered down!
But arguably, cultural differences allow the 'Western nail' to stick up from the floorboard without getting hammered down (at least not at home). I suggest that the incentive for being the 'protruding Western nail' in post-modern Karate is the ability to engage in 'Creative Interpretation', and be recognised.

Innovation *under the guise of tradition* is a common practice, particularly in less flexible social environs. However, an MMA fighter by contrast has little of such matters to be concerned with, and no 'tradition' to protect whilst trying to unravel kata.

Some of my critics, those wedded to 'Creative Interpretation', can see only 'proscriptive dogmatism' in my challenge to it – 'Johnson-ism' perhaps. Yet, their own views seem somewhat entrenched:
> ...as I don't believe the theory and wont buy the book, pretty much makes me redundant in this thread..[.] As I mentioned earlier, I could have a written letter

from the kata's original creator stating its original purpose and I'll still say they missed the point... (King 2006).

Such critics habitually grade or value my research using the very type of dogmatic approach (one faceted) they accuse me of wanting to impose. Further, challenging the existing model seems only to elicit a response drawn from *within* that model, for example: "Why does Johnson think his 'interpretation' is better than mine - or my teacher's?" Indeed their overarching concern seems to be *who* is right, not, *what* is right.

As I have said, I largely reject the 'Creative Interpretation' model, despite the fact that my books *Zen Shaolin Karate* and *Barefoot Zen* contained elements of it; principally speculation on connections with Chan/Zen Buddhism, pushing-hands, and the suggestion that *all* kata were for grappling. My research was incomplete at that point.

In the following section, I will briefly describe my research premise.

Simple Research Paradigms

The Naihanchin application-discovery provided evidence that challenged the 'Creative Interpretation' model. It led directly to my recognising that the antique/ancient kata were not multi-faceted, multi-layered 'magical formulae' and 'panacea for all ills', but were rather workaday drills, routines with specific (and limited) intentions behind each and every physical movement.

I calculated this by testing a simple hypothesis:
What if a given movement in a kata was the result of (the opponent's *limited response* to) the movement that preceded it? That would go some way to explaining kata order. But 'such' would require a swift tactical reduction of the opponent's capabilities, and that quickly achieved, (limiting/controlling the free movement of his arms). This is actually a common combat phenomenon when the combatants are evenly matched, (not the common deference shown to a master by a student) and when protagonists are *genuinely* competing with each other.

For example, in MMA, distances get quickly closed, often followed by the inevitable 'takedown', and attempts at 'the mount' - straddling and then pinning the opponent - technique choices will be limited. However, in respect of formulating unarmed kata, the permutations possible in the mêlée *before the grappling* are too many to put into a meaningful ballistic/percussive-based *sequence*, BECAUSE THERE IS NOTHING HERE TO DETERMINE THE ORDER! The assumption that this range, and these circumstances are what kata portray, is, in my view, probably the most widespread and elementary modern/post-modern error in terms of understanding kata arrangement, function, and value. It is also one of the largest *theoretical* source pools for 'Creative Interpretation'. I suggest free-sparring (kickboxing style) is a more suitable attitude/approach to take in respect of a pre grappling mêlée – the exchange of punches kicks, feints, menaces and tactics.

The existence of fixed moves, full steps, formal upright positions (no ducking, bobbing and weaving, or ground-fighting) and stop start techniques that are of themselves ORDERLY, do not represent, nor can they cope with a disorganised pre-contact mêlée; meaning, there is no stopping cage-fighter Chuck Lidell (or those who supersede him) in full flight by using a 'sword hand' block!

According to my findings therefore, kata application is what happens largely once contact has been made and a degree of control has been, *or is being*, established.

Pre-emptive cross-tying arms in Naihanchin, or 'hooking' the opponents *sword and scabbard,* using the sai for examples, would create the limits and controls that can determine and help catalogue the continuing responses, (should they be necessary) and thus create a clear order for kata, making logical sequences of events *objective requirements, rather than subjective choices.* I do not infer here that the subjugation of an opponent requires the use of an entire kata.

To reiterate: this means that the employment of pre-emptive actions will limit responses and *delineate* the permutations, once any distance is closed, contact is made, and primary 'checking' or prevention is achieved; i.e. stopping a sword from being drawn, rather than dealing with it once it has been drawn.

A second hypothesis I developed suggests that (Uechi Sanchin) like Naihanchin [1, 2&3] is in three parts and that for both kata, the first section represents the basic technique - the essential techniques - with the following sections officering variants that require a complete understanding of the first section.

Naihanchin has 'borne out' these hypotheses admirably, and the reason for its *specific* order became clear. Finally, understanding its pre-emptive context (civil arrest in a bygone era) provided me with a research tool with which I could measure the validity of other kata.

In the following section I employ 'Occam's razor' as a method of rhetorical expression or parallel. I do so to indicate why I *reject* the notion that a single Karate kata can be used with or without weapons.

Occam's razor - The Fewest Assumptions

Q. What is the Connection between a duck and a prison sentence? Before attempting an answer, let's try to establish what a duck is.

"If it looks like a duck, walks like a duck, quacks like a duck, it's a duck! (Simplified application of Occam's razor)

Interpolation!
But… could it be a goose? Or even a swan?

Development:
"**Swans** are birds of the family, Anatidae which also includes **geese** and **ducks**. Swans are grouped with the closely related geese in the subfamily Anserinae where they form the tribe **Cygnini**. Sometimes, they are considered a distinct subfamily, **Cygninae**…" (Wikipedia., Swan, anon, no date).

So, a duck can be a swan (family member), which is also a kind of *bird*, surely? Perhaps 'Googling' 'bird' will clarify, or produce a fresh set of 'ideas'?

'Bird' is a colloquialism for 'time served in prison', a vernacular term for a girlfriend, a satellite in orbit, or a warm blooded, hollow boned, feathered animal. Taking the 'principle' that satisfies our original question (which includes the term 'prison') and rejecting the rest, we can conclude that a duck and a prison sentence are related, and even perhaps that one *develops* from the other, and is, in principle, inherent in it.

I could thus argue contiguously, that, a single kata *was designed to be used with **and** without weapons,* and in many different ways and at several levels, against one or multiple opponents… (See Conclusion B for a final point regarding this). It seems supporters of such a theory are happy to consider such, when 'mysterious' Oriental kata are under consideration. However, if I were to suggest, for example, that a fifteenth century English broadsword-drill could be applied both with, and without the sword, and further, that it would also 'mysteriously' contribute to my horse-riding skills, my suggestions would most likely invoke guffaws of laughter, or frowns at the very least.
'Creative Interpretation' of kata perpetuates the 'mystery' of Karate. New layers (read levels) of applications can, when required, be gleaned from the same old (hackneyed) source material – The Karate kata 'Swiss Army knife'!

I concur that some interpreters of kata are remarkably creative and they and their creations have a certain appeal. However, because few have thought 'outside of the box' (at least for a long time), my work, or rather, *research conclusions,* are immediately challenged under the 'freedom of creativity' *unwritten rules*, applied by most interpreters of Karate kata. And that's even before the sceptics become involved…

Non-engagement with Invisible 'Cyber Critics'

A little indirect hostility (towards me) follows below. I use the word indirect, because I have never, personally, at any point (and still have not) posted or even advertised on a forum. I do not run the Ko-do Ryu website, and I have never asked another individual to post or speak for me on the web.

Morris Takes Internet too seriously Reged: 11/04/05 Posts: 6600	📖**Re: Kodoryu** [Re: _butterfly_] #15894462 – 10/25/06 08:20 PM
	it's gets even more suspect. _http://www.youtube.com/watch?v=TsXj8NJHSxg_ brainstormed idea: lets take uechi ryu kata (which is a rarety in the UK, so now the brits have been scrambling for it in the past decade) and add kobudo weapons to it...and lets say we do it that way, because kata is intended for weapons. ...that outta sell. 😊 {shakes his head and walk away} Post Extras: 📋 🐾 🚫

(Morris 2006).

My challenge, my 'going against the grain', so to speak, not surprisingly, has led (among other things) to charges of dogmatism, elitism, arrogance and even profiteering being laid at my door. So, for clarity I will state here:

I am not directly challenging thousands upon thousands of Karate practitioners personally. Nor am I challenging the personal fighting ability, toughness, fitness, or personal experience of those working, (for example), as doormen. _Indeed, many feel they have successfully applied 'principles' of their own devising or 'principles' created by others, based on the 'Creative Interpretation' of kata model. I am not challenging that or their integrity either_, I am merely challenging the prevalent model of thinking, not for fun, not on a blog, or web-chat, not for vanity, or for money, but for knowledge - ever mindful of the gravity the subject deserves.

Knowing full well that many modern and post-modern Karate teachers, and experts, have enjoyed much of their success based on the 'Creative Interpretation' model, and that their values and belief systems are, as I have suggested, dominant, my task has been made doubly difficult.

This paper represents the culmination of thirty-six years of experience and twenty years of research. In 'decoding' the kata discussed here, I have suffered the same sense of 'loss' as some of my readers, colleagues and associates (from a number of disciplines); those who have understood the implications of my research. Dreams have been shattered, cherished beliefs discarded, Karate kata were not designed to carry a Zen message. Long valued, trusted, enigmatic antique/ancient kata, - nothing but obsolete drills for civil arrest tools? No more mystery, no 'secret powers', delayed death touch - not even unarmed self defence.

I have worked on, edited and published 'over three hundred and fifty thousand words on Karate and related arts, but it has been difficult to formulate ways of communicating my major findings as they grew and changed. Indeed, many 'cyber experts' seemed unable or unwilling to engage in sensible debate, choosing instead to fixate on who my teachers were, my age, the kanji (Japanese Characters) my (Japanese) publishers chose for Naihanchin, in my first book; the price of my books (beyond my control) etc.

Others have bemoaned the fact that I chose to publish the results of a three year *full time unfunded writing project* in a book, rather than engaging in 'cyber space' forum debates to experience (I believe the terms are)' flaming and trolling'? Despite the fact that I had (at that time) no internet access, or desire to use it.

Anyone online and even remotely interested in my work received the customary 'initiation' (flaming?) at the hands of a limited number of people, as some included records will show. Unfortunately, I am reminded of the school yard here:

Ed_Morris is Ed_Morris	┚**Re: Kodoryu** [Re: *butterfly*] #15894459 - 10/25/06 07:57 PM	▯▯▯▯
Reged: 11/04/05 Posts: 6619	wow! ALL the secrets in one book! 😊 you be smellin what I be smellin?...{sniff}{sniff}... A-Gen-Da! blanketed in a recycled hot pocket of steaming B.S. Post Extras: 👍 🐾 🚫	

(Morris 2006).

According to Jenny Block (2008), such behaviour is common on internet forums:
> People can be so cruel, especially on the web. Sometimes I think it's the primary thing for which people use the Internet -- to exercise their dark side.
> The Internet has made it possible for anyone to write, for anyone to share an opinion. And that's fabulous. The thing is it doesn't necessarily get people involved in any kind of real discussion. Sure there's some talking. But I'm not

convinced that there's enough listening or thinking or processing. The problem is that it's simply too easy to be hateful towards or dismiss someone you don't know, someone who you can't see, someone whose story, despite their bio and writing, is basically a mystery to you.

It's like some sort of open invitation -- "Let the flaming, lurking, and trolling begin...

Indeed, in my experience, detractors were most unkind, and the term 'flaming' was indeed used in a post connected to the 'thread' under discussion; although the poster expected that treatment himself.

Finally, during the various exchanges, the mediating, words of Sensei Steve Rowe of Shi Kon Budo came online, (Rowe 2006). Steve is one of Britain's most senior Martial Artists. He holds an 8th dan in Karate; is a columnist for Martial Arts Illustrated, a former columnist for Traditional Karate and is the Chairman of the National Martial Arts Standards Agency.

Steve has hosted numerous well attended courses that I have run. He is one of the most open minded informal but no nonsense sensei in the UK. Steve is extremely skilful, highly qualified, very experienced, and a good friend,

Bossman Veteran	Re: Kodoryu [Re: Unsu] #15896045 - 10/31/06 11:51 AM	
Reged: 08/25/03 Posts: 1780 Loc: Chatham Kent UK	Blimey - thought I was on the Shi Kon Forum there.... 😊 I've known Nathan Johnson for nearly 20 years and have watched him train, research and grow over that period of time. He helped me a lot about 15 years ago with my research into pushing hands. He came from a Wing Chun and Karate base and is a natural researcher. If you put his name into an amazon search engine you will see that he has authored and co-authored many books on a variety of subjects, all well researched and over a long period of time. Nathan and I disagree on many things in the Martial Arts and that's what helps bond our friendship - we're allowed to disagree and be grown up. Like most academics he researches, publishes and moves on - he doesn't even have a particular interest in the controvesy and certainly hasn't asked anyone to 'argue his case'. Also like all academics (and the bulk of us MA instructors) he certainly ain't rich! If you can go train with him do so, we had him for a course recently on the subject of the book and my guys thoroughly	

> enjoyed it as 'something different' to what we usually do.
>
> He's a real character, loves academia and martial arts, a bit of a hermit, hard to get in touch with and doesn't have access to the internet. He doesn't even know what's on his website and is already immersed in another project.
>
> I think Tom just likes a good argument, I'm the opposite in character to Nathan yet we can meet up, often with Chris Rowen the goju practitioner, have lunch, talk martial crap, exchange ideas, have a laugh and go our seperate ways.
>
> And we've remained good friends for a long time.
>
> --------------------
> supporting standards in the martial arts
> *www.shikon.com*
> *www.masa.org.uk*

Well, I hope the 'flaming and trolling' (or whatever it is) will hopefully move on to the next forum topic (target). In the meantime, I will return to the subject proper.

Throughout this paper, I strongly suggest that post-modern Western values and attitudes are now at work in interpreting kata that were already enigmatic to, for example, the nineteenth century Okinawan Karate practitioners - early Karate progenitors - the people who gave Karate its name, yet who were, and until recently have remained, *notoriously ambivalent regarding practical combative applications for kata.*

Nagamine Shoshin, informs us:

> There are as many theories concerning the origins and executions of the kata as there are schools of karate. Some have theorized, for example, that the movements of the kata derived from mimicking the protective movements of animals. Others have speculated that the kata grew out of ancient dance forms...Unfortunately, the lack of a comprehensive theory of the movements and how they are executed results in less interest in simple practice of the basic movements of the kata (Nagamine 1976. p. 56).

This suggests that early Okinawan kata enthusiasts found the Chinese solo forms to be cryptic and impenetrable themselves. Limited applications for kata that began to appear on Okinawa during the nineteenth century were devised much later than the actual kata themselves.

Indeed, as I have suggested, the current frenetic demand for applications has largely occurred since the exposure of Karate to Western functional mindsets. Not inculcated into filial piety, unprepared to wait long years, and dissatisfied with abstract or convoluted explanations for kata, Occidentals, modern Westernised Orientals and others (many of whom have studied with the 'masters' since the 1960's) have postulated their own 'interpretations', which are, as I have suggested, sometimes at odds with those they have been taught by their mentors.

Personally I find post-modern creative interpretations far more attractive than the 'modern' 'face value' and somewhat crude and literal punch, block, strike, kick applications that grew out of the post WW2 era (the notorious JKA Bunkai series for example). This is at the heart of the matter and has contributed to the problem (belief system) of 'multiple applications' of movements in kata. Early applications were (remain) primitive – many people felt they could do better, and have.

For example Pat McCarthy, has created a post-modern theorem which is, in my view, head and shoulders above the 'it can be anything you want it to be' market-driven 'free-for-all'. Mr McCarthy has detractors (which I suggest is healthy) but more insidiously, imitators who do not acknowledge sources but plagiarise his ideas; that group is growing into a phalanx!

As a fiercely independent researcher, if I (and this is not my alter ego speaking), were a Samurai warrior, I would be a Ronin, a master-less Samurai. Therefore I am not in Mr McCarthy's camp, or anyone else's. However, Pat McCarthy has put forward a proper 'theorem' a model or formulae, in keeping with promoting the ethos of authentic Ryu. I commend his H.A.P.V (habitual acts of violence formulae) whilst not embracing it. My interests lie elsewhere, and lean toward very specific kata and the implications of their application and context.

Returning to the 'free for all' mentioned earlier, I suggest that the very (post-modern) approach of 'Creative Interpretation', logically and inevitably has lead to the escalation of pseudo kata and will eventually lead to the virtual redundancy, or abandonment of the antique/ancient kata, except perhaps by those predisposed to the arcane, or loyal to a style that practices them. I mean here, Karate as we think we know it is not about to be discarded immediately, but the 'writing could well be on the wall'.

Consider the increasing popularity of MMA as an example. Indeed, it is ever more common for modern styles to decry the lack of practical value in kata and eschew them completely. And this group is growing – fast!

MMA has already eroded Karate's market. Graphic, violent, and satisfying curiosity regarding actual confrontational fighting, MMA is real, it's present, it's accessible, and much 'higher octane' than allegorical stories about old Okinawan Karate masters who won or lost duels, depending on which one adopted the most powerful 'ready stance', all without a blow being exchanged!

Social traditions and behaviours are changing. Youth continues to rebel (increasingly so in Japan), the old is giving way to the new. Karate is losing its monopoly – Western and other cultures have become more graphic, more visceral. Information is now at the fingertips of the many and not the few. In short you can view legends like Funakoshi Gichin of Karate, or Yip Man (Bruce Lee's formal Kung Fu teacher) on-line for yourself, and compare them with contemporary masters, or cage fighters, or anyone you choose. The myths that inspired previous generations are losing their grip. New myths beckon! But the kata remain – 'enigmatic messages in movement'.

Seminal kata from the world's major Karate styles are fully discussed in my publications and subjected to new methodologies of interpretation. My main assertion is that their purpose was to record and (perhaps clandestinely) disseminate the use of weapons, originally in a cultural environment that rigidly controlled the ownership, display and use of weapons amongst a people or race (the indigenous Han race) subjugated by the Manchu's after the fall of the important and regionally influential 'Ming' dynasty in 1644.

It is commonly stated that kata is at the heart of true Karate, yet when put to, what many consider to be the litmus test for an unarmed so called 'fighting art', i.e. actual combat - they fail quite miserably for reasons I document here.

In the next section I will appraise my three relevant publications, and make brief critical reflections. I will also supply relevant personal background material pertaining to practical experience, and try to illustrate how difficult it is to challenge widely held misconceptions generally, and with respect to Karate - specifically.

Chapter Two

The Substance of my three Publications

In *Zen Shaolin Karate* I explored the idea that the 'original kata' were associated with the Chan Buddhism of China and later the Zen schools of Japan. Zen is the Japanese interpretation/pronunciation of the Chinese term 'Channa' which was in turn a Chinese pronunciation of the Indian word Dyhanna – meditation.
The technical material in the book included a hybrid Sanchin kata, my understanding of Naihanchin kata up to and including 1993, and an exposition of pushing hands, which I suggest contributed to a greater awareness and acceptance of pushing hands in mainstream Karate.

I will deviate briefly below in describing some personal experiences that led to the writing of my first book. I do this in a calculated way, as I do not intend this paper to become an autobiography.

Perhaps it will always be challenging to record Karate in prose. That in itself is difficult enough, but when ones views seem so radical, then there is a second difficulty. It was indeed very challenging to get my work published (26 refusals), but it was finally accepted by one of the most prestigious publishers of Martial Arts books in the world. My editor, Alexander Kask, congratulated me with a, 'Well done!' He went on to suggest that only 'real experts', or those who had sat at the feet of Oriental masters for years, ever got published by Tuttle. I confess I felt like neither.

Many readers, peers, and commentators (see book reviews) enjoyed my interpretation of the famous Sanchin kata (from The Naha city tradition - Okinawa), yet I was still very much involved in modern and post-modern attitudes and beliefs regarding the function of kata.

For example, at the time of my beginning serious research in 1988, I still believed that Sanchin was a method of unarmed combat. Most people did. Why would I think anything else? Besides, the 'hsing' of Chinese Kung Fu, were also considered to be unarmed combat routines or drills too, and Sanchin *was* from China. Moreover, I had trained extensively in Chinese Kung Fu and was, putting it mildly, an enthusiast.

As late as 1992 I had still not considered the possibility of Karate kata being *solely* weapons drills, but I had begun to give up on the idea of Sanchin being a practical means of cataloguing anything other than 'ritual combat', and I had already begun to think, "No matter how much of a 'sacred cow' Sanchin is, no matter how well regarded it has become and no matter how many hundreds of thousands of people practice it worldwide, it's still a peculiar way to prepare for a 'no holds barred' fight."

When I was first taught Sanchin in the late 1970's and early 1980's I believed that I was learning something ancient, something profound, something that had been handed down from antiquity. I was wrong! In fact, I learned the popular version created by the celebrated founder of Goju Ryu Karate, Miyagi Chojun. He had 'refined' Sanchin in the same year my mother was born – not that that's necessarily a bad thing.[2]

Many enthusiasts claimed that kata could be anything one wanted them to be or nothing at all. Others insisted kata had a purpose. Many masters and experts (no end of them, it seemed) insisted that standing in Sanchin's peculiar knock-kneed pigeon-toed stance and practicing the kata many times over, would, (without any sensible applications) be good preparation for combat. There was a *just do it* attitude at that time.

To this day it is considered improper by many practitioners of Sanchin kata to desire applications. To do so is to risk being shunned as an iconoclast.

Indeed, thinking of icon's, Bruce Lee, the Kung Fu expert and film star had openly questioned the validity of 'forms' (hsing/kata) and had outright rejected them during the late 1960's, denouncing them in private letters and famously in his notes, posthumously published as *The Tao of Jeet Kune Do* in 1976.

Dan Inasanto, one of Bruce Lees top students (and a very close friend of Lee's) told me (D Inasanto, *pers. comm.*, Giko 2, 1984) that Bruce Lee discarded 'forms' on the grounds that they restricted the fluidity of a fighter and were, and I quote, "...pretty much useless and just for show."

Western boxing and wrestling don't have kata, yet no one questions their efficiency, they are just seen as different 'beasts'. Why is that? I wondered.

However, my speculations were not simply based on philosophic musings. Whilst I am not now going to 'perjure' myself, so to speak, and present myself as a tough veteran of X number of brutal gladiatorial combats, I did experience a steep learning curve when I 'touched gloves' with one of Britain's up and coming light heavyweight boxers. That experience and several like it (plus a few without rules or protective equipment) contributed to my 'rethink' about Kung Fu and related arts. All despite the fact that I was in superb physical condition, as several people on the acknowledgements page can attest. Various arranged 'fights' I engaged in were often inconclusive and undignified events during which neither party seemed able to use the techniques (read format) we had trained so hard in. The traditional 'stuff' just didn't seem to work in the rough and tumble of no rules combat. Incidentally and in respect of the calibre of my opposition, I was involved in the famous Wing Chun challenge matches of the 1980's.

---

[2] Miyagi Sanchin, (like Itosu's five Pinan/Heian kata) is a synthetic kata. In my view, I consider it to have no proper applications because it is, in essence, a modified Sai kata.

Away from Wing Chun, one of my most notable opponents was an incumbent middleweight European semi-contact champion. That was one fight I won – conclusively and very quickly. I mean no idle boast here; my opponent was more skilful than I was, but he couldn't use his elegant kicks and point scoring tricks in the rough and tumble of the rugby-tackle spoiling tactics I brought to bear. All this was at least fourteen years before UFC, etc. However, a good example of what I discuss here can be found on YouTube – Rhodes vs. Etish – Extreme Sports. A Caveat is in order here - it does *not* make pleasant viewing!

Always more of a sportsman than a fighter, and having had the benefit of a good education I felt ashamed after the bout I described above. But after my (hollow) victory, a small crowd of 'mates' slapped me on the back and turned any chance of conversation/de-brief into an immediate quest for beer.

Like Bruce Lee, I began to doubt the usefulness of hsing/kata. Perhaps, unlike Bruce Lee, I remained fascinated by them. I was captivated by a number of related questions, so much so that I was obliged to try to clarify my thoughts on paper. What was the purpose of the enigmatic, ritualised sequences of Martial Arts moves? Was something being hidden? Were there secrets? These and other thoughts I had on the subject, were hardly original. In fact they were rather commonplace. However, when an acquaintance reminded me of the connection between the Chinese Martial Arts and the Shaolin Temple, I decided to investigate Buddhism to find some answers, and a new direction or path seemed to 'open up'.

I now find it most peculiar to be responsible for de-bunking the very 'mythologies' that kept me interested in Kung Fu and Karate. But that indeed is what I have set out to do in my publications, and again here.

All researchers face criticism and even open hostility. Nicholas Copernicus is an excellent example. I do not mean here to associate myself with him by proxy. However, there are similarities in the sense of the huge numbers of people whose beliefs are challenged, and that's before the responses of 'those in authority' and with a vested interest in preserving the status quo.

The following model is my own creation:
Assumption 1)
Everyone sees the sun rise in the east and set in the west, ergo, the sun goes around the earth – every sighted person can see that!
Refutation
Nicholas Copernicus 1473 – 1543 was the first astronomer to describe a scientifically based sun-centered universe that displaced the Earth from the center of the universe.
Assumption 2)
Everyone knows that Karate is a deadly form of unarmed Martial Arts, ergo, its kata delineate unarmed combat – every sighted person can see that!

Refutation

I describe (Uechi Ryu) old style **Sanchin, Seisan, Sanseriu**, and (Matsubayishi Ryu) **Kusanku** *exclusively as Sai kata* – and (Matsubayishi Ryu) **Naihanchin** *as a two-man grappling form*. These are not just 'any old kata', they are pivotal kata! Insight into their construction provides a key to unlock *many* other antique/ancient kata.

Sanchin, ever considered a seminal kata, was one of the first kata on my list for investigation. It eventually rose to be at the top of the list. By the time I published *The Great Karate Myth* my research had run its course. I discovered that the Uechi (family) *Sanchin, a version indeed considered to be ancient, a version that enjoyed considerable credibility in the Karate circles, was a meticulous and logically crafted solo routine that preserved and yet concealed the very weapons (in this case civil arrest tools) that its choreography reflected*. In short, the reasoning behind the kata, and the order and nuances of it movements, catalogued the methods for successfully manipulating Sai.

Of course opposition was swift and fierce, but it was largely emotional, and, as Dr. Ronnie Ramlogan (a university research fellow and someone who has trained in Karate for over thirty-four years) said: "You have delivered your (sound) case. It is now up to others to respond." And to date, I have read complaints but no comparable theory/refutation, just negation – just, "I don't believe it." Indeed, most of the critics on a popular forum, following a thread that eventually congested that forum, decried my finding, yet openly admitted to having not read *The Great Karate Myth*.

Here is an example from Fighting Arts Forum:

student_of_life the quickness	⬛**Re: Kodoryu** [Re: *cxt*] #15894638 – 10/26/06 11:36 AM	▯▯▯▯
Reged: 10/12/05 Posts: 796 Loc: Newfoundland, Canada	dose it even matter any more what the kata were orioginally intended for? i mean honestly?, i get out of them what i want, im sure wel all do. i don't need to give that guy a nickel to tell me some hair brained conspericy theory about why the kata's meanings were hidden or forgotten or lost. i hope his students enjoy there time with him, 20 years expirence usually means that he knows a thing or two. i really do think that his books are just a gimick to make money, let my flaming begin!! ------------------- Raul Perez - "Take a look, its in a book, reading rainbow." Post Extras: 🖐 🐾 🖉	

('Student of Life' 2006).

And:

Gavin 140lbs of STFU Reged: 05/11/05 Posts: 2059 UK	**Re: Kodoryu** [Re: *kodobrighton2006*] #15894688 - 10/26/06 01:00 PM
	Howdy Tom! See your still fighting the good fight! Wonder as you've been back in the Country are you going to take Mr Rowe up on his offer to show his "interpretations" of the kata's? Anyway we've been through all my opinions on Kodo Ryu stuff and Jim will tell me off if start up here. Anyway nice to see the arguements of the battle haven't changed... merely the battle ground. Where's the next planned battle to be staged? martialartsplanet, e-budo or perhaps Bullshido (you'd have fun there!). Welcome to the forum! A good luck with the agenda... ooops I mean research! Sorry, only joshing! ☺ Gav PS. I still ain't buying the theory or the book though! -------------------- Gavin King

(King 2006).

Fortunately (again):

Bossman Veteran Reged: 08/25/03 Posts: 1780 Loc: Chatham Kent UK	**Re: Kodoryu** [Re: *shoshinkan*] #15896097 - 10/31/06 02:23 PM
	I worked for hours with Nathan at his house and at the university whilst he worked his way through the two handed and one handed grappling, he taught the form and applications on many of my courses I wrote the preface to some of his books and have acknowledgement in the 'Myth'. TBH he'd be horrified at this thread (or probably think everyone was daft) my views? He's brilliant. I love his ideas. They're totally different to mine

and that's why I like them and him.

He gave me a copy of the book and DVD - and I will read it! But meanwhile I quote from the page it just fell open at:
Quote:

I respect the major Karate founders and those honest individuals who have, by the sweat of their brows kept Karate alive, not with a bunch of eccentric flow charts, wacky theories and naive opinions but through sweat and effort in the Dojo

Nathan works with his research in the Dojo and that's why I respect him. I don't think you do him any favours on these forums.

----
supporting standards in the martial arts

Post Extras:

(Rowe 2006).

Returning to the book *Zen Shaolin Karate,* a second seminal kata was illustrated in that book. I worked on it for *over two thousand hours* (capably assisted by Dave Franks and Mathew Tasker).

My findings regarding Naihanchin kata caused enough of a stir to win the support of Pat McCarthy and others.

Zen Shaolin Karate (the publisher's title choice, not mine) postulated that Sanchin kata is central to much Fujianese Kung Fu and to Karate. *It also made the first (coherent) claim for Naihanchin kata - a seminal Shuri City kata, with a long history and a great deal of respect – being, as I have said, a two-man continuous grappling sequence.*

Both Sanchin and Naihanchin kata (featured in the book) are considered to be kata of primary importance. Their Importance was made clear in the 1934 document *Karate Do Gaisetsu* authored by the Karate luminary Miyagi Chojun

Miyagi Chojun

(Okinawan Ryu-ha 'Kihon' Kata were defined by the Karate 'great' Miyagi Chojun (Miyagusuku Chojun, 1888 – 1953) the founder of the popular and now international Goju Ryu Karate style)

In his important 1934 Essay, *Karate Do Gaisetsu*, responsible in part for legitimising Karate with the Japanese authorities, Miyagi states very clearly that the Sanchin, Tensho (Rokushu) and Naihanchi (Naihanchin) kata are the 'kihon' or fundamental kata of the entire Okinawan Karate Ryu-Ha, or (official) Karate 'Martial Tradition'. These kata represent the *two* Ryu (Families/schools) into which Karate is basically divided - Naha-te and Shuri-te.

Barefoot Zen, picks up on the themes of *Zen Shaolin Karate* and takes the research in the direction of moving meditation, complete with a hypothesis to explain how the fabled Shaolin Monks (but known to have existed for real) might have viewed Kung Fu (which is, after all commonly attributed to them) and how that might have reconciled Kung Fu with meditation by creating a kind of 'kinetic meditation' facilitated through the medium of pushing hands.

Limited Chan and Zen Connections

Whilst my own views regarding the Chan. Zen (Shao-lin) genesis of Chinese Martial Arts have shifted considerably since my research for *The Great Karate Myth*, the notion of Chan monks and nuns practicing *pushing hands* does still seem to be feasible. I made my views on the possible associations between Karate and the Shao-lin tradition clear in chapter six of *Barefoot Zen*. The book was written after several years of committed and regular attendance at a major Buddhist monastery where I was fortunate enough to be taken under the wing of the then abbot - 'Ajahn' Anando - and several senior monks (including Ajahn's Kittisaro and Vajiro), and at a time when I feared Karate was descending 'lock stock and barrel' into the (cage fighting) 'pit'.

However, ultimately, I (have had to) conclude that the practical considerations of the antique/ancient kata, outweigh any 'spiritual' content. To be clear here: I *do not confuse pushing hands with kata application*, and my research for *The Great Karate Myth* replaces and disproves my notion that seminal kata were inspired by Chinese religious clerics. My current position is hopefully made clear here.

Barefoot Zen also explores the third kata in Miyagi's kihon kata trilogy – Rokushu, (six hands), more commonly known as 'Tensho' (rotating hands/palms).

Body mechanics were covered extensively in chapter Nine of *Barefoot Zen*. The Basic premise is that all movements in traditional kata are (with a few exceptions) executed within the natural range of movement, something that can clearly be seen in Naihanchin kata. The material on Naihanchin was further refined, and I demonstrated/illustrated the kata as *one long* sequence.

An observer will notice that a Naihanchin performer moves only sideways, and when the alleged three kata (Sho [1] Ni [2] and San [3]) are correctly rejoined (necessary for application), the distance required is approximately the length of tennis court - not much use for the small 'private' courtyards used by early Karate teachers who, it is widely known, taught in secret.

The Great Karate Myth
Once I had established that one of the oldest 'open handed' Sanchin kata, and the base for the version I had previously been studying, was a weapons kata, I felt confident enough to present my finding on the second kata in the Uechi family Karate system – Seisan kata. It proved to be a logical development of the Sanchin kata, and further developed techniques intended to be used with a pair of Sai.

In *The Great Karate Myth* I also turn my attention to other antique/ancient kata and conclude that with the exception of Naihanchin they are all most likely kata designed to teach weapons, principally the Sai. In the next section I will give a brief outline of the Sai.

The Sai

The Sai, a pronged weapon, used in pairs, is quite literally the *key* to understanding many 'classical' so-called Karate kata and their applications, because these kata (open handed Sanchin, Seisan and Kusanku for examples) not only reflect the use of these classical 'tools' but are the exact physical records of how to wield them, how to orient them, and how to manipulate them.

A pair of Sai; a civil arrest tool from China, common also in feudal Okinawa and Japan

Despite its (first impression) appearance, *the Sai is not a stabbing weapon*. The pommel or 'knub' at the top of the handle is the main part of the Sai used in striking. The shaft is occasionally used to 'punish' (the hand that grips a weapon) but is mainly used to protect the user's forearms when the Sai is held (pointing backwards) with the pommel positioned thumb-side of the hand, and also in conjunction with the foil to trap a weapon, when the Sai is used (pointing forward) with the pommel positioned little-finger-side of the hand.

The next section is designed to explore just how and when the meaning and applications of the antique/ancient kata may have been lost. It is general, because there is still much work to be done on this subject. The main body of evidence is founded on accurate kata application, drawn directly from the 'writings in movement'.

The Weapons Ban(s)

Okinawa, the 'home of Karate' has been a vassal state of both China and Japan, and there was undoubtedly a sense of indignation and loss of national pride when their islands were invaded and occupied by the Satsuma clan, and allegedly a weapons ban, for all Okinawans was officially declared in 1609. This may well have been nothing more than a continuation of the status quo. The Okinawans had already been forbidden to bear arms in an edict issued during the reign of the Okinawan King Sho Shin-O (1477-1526).

There was a precedent to these events. Earlier, in China, the hated Mongol invaders successfully established a dynasty there, between 1271 and 1368. They forbade the Chinese Han (race) from owning weapons or even participating in hunting. The Han Chinese people were subject to a curfew, and also restricted in the practice of Martial Arts, religion, and freedom of assembly.

Of the three types of Martial Arts formerly practice by the Han – military, private and theatrical, theatrical Martial Arts (opera style) reached new and unprecedented heights. The Han re-established themselves during the Ming dynasty. But the Manchu's - another non indigenous ethnic group - would impose similar restrictions after the fall of the Ming dynasty in 1644. I strongly suspect that it is during this period that Sanchin, Seisan, Sanseriu, Kusanku and other kata are created – to record, to teach, to maintain and even perhaps to *conceal*. One can't be accused of breaking the weapons ban if there is no weapon in sight!

The type of 'Martial Arts' that these kata derive from are not military or theatrical, but civil and private; police/militia training drills. However, I do not think this to be true for other models of hsing. Wing Chun for example, with its broadsword connection is - in my view – a reflection and distillation of broadsword methods and seems to be (from) a different strain.

The importance of the Sai and related weapons diminished towards the end of the Ming and the beginning of the Ch'ing dynasties (c1644-45). Much of this was due to the large increase in the use of firearms. The Ming was the first dynasty to widely employ gunners, armed with personal weapons, in the ranks of its infantry. Chariots, which had not been used by regular troops since the warring states era (c481-220 AD) made a reappearance, mounted with cannon and used to devastating effect. The size and scale of the conflict in China at that time is beyond the scope of this paper, sufficient to say that the events during the fall of the Ming Dynasty were cataclysmic.

Fortunately, early hsing/kata were transplanted to Okinawa, but not before Okinawa experienced its own problems. Alas, what happened in Ming dynasty China had happened on Okinawa in 1609 (as noted). It is well known that the small but well-armed and combat-experienced Satsuma Samurai treated the native Okinawans with contempt and brutality, and this may have, in part, fuelled an interest in what appeared to be an empty hand art amongst young Okinawans. However, To-te (lit', China hand – later Karate) does not appear on Okinawa much before the end of the eighteenth century and the beginning of the nineteenth century. It was nearly two hundred years after the Satsuma invasion/subjugation of Okinawa that named Okinawans like Kanga Chikudon 'Pechin' Teruya, better known as To-te Sakugawa, 1782-1862, (some sources claim 1733-1815), are recorded as To-te (Karate) practitioners.

Unfortunately, fundamental breakdowns in the transmission of the purpose for key (antique/ancient) kata have occurred with the passing of time. Since the seventeenth century, war, disease, cultural devastation and radical political reforms have befallen Southern China, the birthplace of and the cradle of hsing/kata later to be utilised and 'adapted' to create Okinawan Karate. At that time, it seems many traditions were lost or distorted. During the eighteenth and nineteenth centuries Okinawa suffered similarly too. With her population weakened by poverty and disease and decimated by the ravages of the pacific war, and with her cities and infrastructure bombed virtually flat during that period, Okinawan cultural confidence hit an all time low and the development of Karate suffered a significant setback. Consequently, much needed (specific) research into the its home-grown, *imported,* and seemingly cryptic kata, could not be properly undertaken, let alone concluded before the art was exported far beyond the borders of the former Japanese Empire.

Chapter Three, defines my understanding of Karate kata generally, and (the) antique/ancient kata specifically.

Chapter Three

Grappling and Civil Arrest

I suggest that the armed *civil arrest* nature and intent of the antique/ancient kata accounts for their exotic appearance and is a major reason for the confusion regarding applications. This is either an historic misunderstanding, or a deliberate adaptation.

Indeed, it is the case that some (modern) kata were not constructed for practical application at all, being constructed instead for martial display, exercise, the cultivation of general martial 'bearing' and to provide a culturally-based physical education curriculum for Okinawan schoolchildren; one that would, within twenty years of its inception, be adopted by mainland Japanese university students.

It is likely that kata created or modified during the last century were constructed or adapted on the *assumption* that the original source material found in the Chinese prototypes represented a weapon-less, unarmed art. But, at work here is one, or at the most, two possibilities: ignorance or concealment. Ignorance insomuch as the weapon-based function of many kata may have been unknown to the early (Okinawan) inheritors of Chinese hsing, or, the total concealment of the fact that the antique/ancient hsing - from which many Karate kata were created - were originally weapons kata.

Karate has now reached such large worldwide audiences that *several millions* of modern Karate practitioners are now asking the sorts of questions that, in the main, were largely *unasked* by *several hundred* Okinawan practitioners of *early* To-te.

Traditionally, those who 'questioned' were reproached with admonitions such as, train harder/faster, trust tradition, or, 'one day you will understand'. However, an un-attributed source suggests:
"*Insanity is doing the same thing over and over, whilst expecting different results.*"
(Anonymous: variously attributed to Einstein, Rita Mae Brown, Rudyard Kipling, and others)

So far, I have suggested much that constitutes supposed weapon-less kata-based Karate was predicated either unwittingly or wittingly upon techniques originally designed to be used with weapons. It is also timely here to re-visit Naihanchin (Tekki 1, 2&3).

My work has made it mainstream knowledge that Naihanchin is a primary Shuri-te kata, (of Chinese origin) comprising of techniques that catalogue double-armed grappling procedures, seemingly designed to completely subdue and restrain an opponent via the twisting of wrist joints, and the 'locking' of elbow joints, to 'arrest' that opponent.

In China, grappling techniques were known as Chi-na (to seize and grapple, pronounced 'chee – naa') where I suggest they were used to make unarmed arrests.

NB. The use of the term 'arrest' does not imply that the person being 'arrested' is necessarily a criminal as such, but just that their movement (and therefore their immediate liberty) is arrested, stopped, brought under control.

In the penultimate section (before my conclusion) I re-link the arts of Sai and of grappling, and provide a rudimentary social context.

Grappling and the Sai – The Connection

In *The Great Karate Myth*, I suggest that Chi-na originally underpinned a 'civil arrest' tradition that utilised Sai to disarm and arrest an armed offender, with the emphasis on preventing the drawing of, for example, a sword, and 'seizing and grappling' techniques designed to subdue and arrest an offender before he could draw a weapon and escalate hostility. All accomplished without killing or maiming.

Indeed, this would suggest that the operatives did not hold the right to simply cut down offenders. In parallel, in Japan the Samurai did hold that right, and salacious history insists that they used it.

I suggest that the objective for a (non high status) civil arrest officer was to detain an individual according to established protocols and procedures, and to render up that individual in a fit condition to be questioned, possibly to face trial and or formal punishment. I contest that this was unquestionably a civil matter and not a military one, even though it must have involved or included members of the military too. Also, the 'arrestee' may well be a social superior, so appropriate 'treatment' would be essential; (his family might own the land your family lives on). I do not rule out here the simple arrest of a drunk, or a criminal.

I am clear that the social context was quite unlike that found where a national policing system operates. The methods used and described above, were intended for use on behalf of the civil authorities and most likely pertained only to tackling and resolving incidences, as I have said, under civil jurisdiction and that most likely being feudal or semi feudal in nature.

The next section concludes this paper with two strongly made points. It is preceded by an informal summary of one of my main topics of discussion; the 'Creative Interpretation of Kata'.

Conclusion

I can now conclude that the sheer number of modern and post-modern variations in Karate kata application, ('Creative Interpretation') *evidences* profound uncertainties regarding the functions of the antique/ancient kata, and the role/value of kata in actual fighting:

Kata choices become problematic. Seekers can't see the wood for the trees, as more and more kata 'appear' with increasingly diverse theories to match. Enthusiasts and doubters alike, express difficulty in determining which kata (formats) are original. *The very idea of original kata is frequently, but mistakenly, lambasted*, in favour of a 'no such thing' insistence. Yet, I reiterate, there is much confusion uncertainty, doubt, and plain lack of consistency in respect of kata application. If that's what the creators intended, they did a fine job, if not...

"Kata are not fixed! Cry the 'Interpreters'. They are 'fluid', always changing." So say those who seem unable to recognise the equivalent of a bayonet drill, a fire drill, or any drill – nothing exists for these people, all is in flux and never stays still for long enough to be identified – particularly hsing/kata! I remind readers of that very attitude:

student_of_life the quickness	📖 **Re: Kodoryu** [Re: *cxt*] #15894638 – 10/26/06 11:36 AM
Reged: 10/12/05 Posts: 796 Loc: Newfoundland, Canada	dose it even matter any more what the kata were orioginally intended for? i mean honestly?, i get out of them what i want, im sure wel all do. i don't need to give that guy a nickel to tell me some hair brained conspericy theory about why the kata's meanings were hidden or forgotten or lost. i hope his students enjoy there time with him, 20 years expirence usually means that he knows a thing or two. i really do think that his books are just a gimick to make money, let my flaming begin!! -------------------- Raul Perez - "Take a look, its in a book, reading rainbow." Post Extras: 🍺 🐾 ⊘

('Student of Life' 2006).

I do not feel the need to assure my readers that my experience, research and publications, are no 'gimmick'. However, I stake the time spent, and my reputation, on the following statement: In respect of Uechi, Sanchin, Seisan, Sanseriu, along with Naihanchin and Kusanku; I contest that *the founders of these kata knew precisely what they purposed, and recorded such with unerring accuracy*, and that those purposes are stated in this paper.

In the meantime, I suggest 'Creative Interpretation' remains stuck in its self-created 'assumptions' which have, and will inevitably, lead to more 'Creative Interpretation(s)'.

I further suggest, that post-modern 'Creative Interpretation' of kata *requires*, and therefore *insists*, that there are (essentially pre-existing) unarmed ballistic-based kata of 'never ending' permutations; applications that act as trans-cultural paradigms of attack and defence, etc.

'Creative Interpretation' insists that such were constructed for, or can be modified to, cope with the problems of 'anything goes' random barehanded violence, (today or at anytime in history). Or that such can even now be constructed. I dispute this and say, in a statement related to the title of this paper; *the more such 'interpretations' become effective, the more they will resemble MMA, and not the antique/ancient kata,* with further (inevitable) changes made to those kata.

Moreover, I am convinced that post-modern kata have no 'proper' applications, because they are largely modified or created under false assumptions (developed in the main, out of weapons kata). Creative Interpretation' is then, in my final analysis, the *least useful methodology* when applied to the antique/ancient kata in terms of 'application'.

Therefore:

A) I refute 'Creative Interpretation' of the antique/ancient Kata on the strength of my research, which suggests that context is vital. For example, Naihanchin could only be truly 'effective' if used for its original purpose, i.e. its application in the *appropriate cultural and environmental situation*; one in which, perhaps, an antagonist was, at the least, about to become unruly, was already unruly, or was moving towards *drawing a weapon*.

B) Finally, one-to-one confrontation, the most common focus of attention (debate etc) in Karate, is most likely highlighted because of the 'target audience', children, young (predominantly male) adults, and thereafter people interested in personal self defence who comprise the hub around which 'Creative Interpretation' revolves. *I contend that there is nothing that proves, or even suggests, that the antique/ancient methods were ever intended or used for individual personal 'self defence'* in the manner commonly perceived, or that the kata applications were intended for solo use, even though 'engagement' is between pairs. I doubt that the Naihanchin operator, or the Sai operator, worked alone. I think, just like the 'Bobbies on Bicycles' of old 'Blighty', they went *two by two*. Or, even as now, had lots of backup! For example, the two 'lock up' points in Naihanchin application most likely exist as places where a colleague can tie the subjugated person with rope. And, an errant swordsman may well have found himself facing two or more Sai operatives. *This is precisely the reverse ratio* to that which modern Karate practitioners imagine when they consider a scene involving multiple combatants.

Appendix

Plaudits

Book ONE:
Johnson, N.J. 1994. Zen Shaolin Karate: The Complete Practice. Tokyo: Tuttle 1994

Selected Plaudits (Publishers and Peers)

"Nathan Johnson has captured the essence of true karate-do."
- Paul Clifton, Editor Combat and Traditional Karate (front cover Zen Shaolin Karate)

"Entirely original and convincing research, an argument that has profound and lasting implications for the study and teaching of Karate Today".
Peter Eagle. Kodansha Europe - Far Eastern Publishers (Kodansha distribution literature Sept 1994)

"...Johnson's approach is fascinating and original and should provoke some serious soul searching about the directions martial arts (Karate) is taking, and the aims and attitudes of its practitioners."
The Daily Yomiuri (Broadsheet), Tokyo Japan - Sunday May 15th 1994

"Nathan Johnson discoveries are nothing short of illuminating, and will unquestionably throw a new perspective (old perspective) on an obscure art which already has 'too much'. More plausible than anything I have seen yet."
Patrick McCarthy. 7th Dan Karate (Butokukai granted Kyoshi grade) Karate Director of International Rykyu Karate Research Group (McCarthy's European tour seminar notes July 1995 - supplied Aug 1995 - appears on the draft cover of Barefoot Zen, but replaced by Weiser)

Concerning Naihanchin bunkai - I found it to be excellent work when I saw it in Sussex. The techniques are well evolved and possibly close to the originals.
Mark Bishop. 7th Dan Karate (Jundokan Honbu, Okinawa) author of *Okinawan Karate: Teachers Styles and Secret Techniques* (supplied Aug 1995 and appears on draft cover of Barefoot Zen, but replaced by Weiser)

Zen Shaolin Karate (continued)
General Plaudits

The following reviews were taken from the Amazon website *http://www.amazon.co.uk* between July 30th 2008 and September 8th 2008. They have been archived.

Affirmation

I, Nathan J. Johnson affirm and confirm, (to the best of my knowledge) that I do not know, nor have I ever met or communicated directly, or indirectly, with any of the reviewers whose comments follow below, (other than by virtue of the fact that they have read my books). This, of course, excludes Patrick McCarthy.

Superb Interpretations of Sanchin and Naihanchi, December 29, 2002
By *C. J. Hardman* (San Diego, CA USA) - *See all my reviews*
REAL NAME™

The title of this book, "Zen Shaolin Karate" unfortunately conjures the image of an Americanized kenpo style. Nothing is farther from the truth--Author Nathan Johnson offers a superb interpretation of two of the most widely practiced fundamental kata (forms) of Okinawa Karate, the Sanchin Kata of Goju Ryu, and the Naihanchi Kata of Shorin-ryu. Johnson has researched these two forms, and reconstructed them as he believes they were performed before being altered to teach to the masses. We see for the first time in an English language publication, Sanchin performed open handed. Naihanchin is presented as one complete form in three parts (as researchers believe it was performed prior to Itosu's time). For both forms, bunkai emphasizing locking and grappling is demonstrated, including close up photos showing how the locks are performed.

Johnson is in essence, apparently attempting to reintroduce the older Chinese methods of study, a growing trend among some Okinawa Karate stylists. My one sticking point with this book is Johnson's lack of bibliographic sources, he isn't very specific about how he did his research and how he reached his conclusions. What were his influences, who did he talk to, who did he study with, what articles and volumes did he read? Johnson's second volume, "Barefoot Zen" does much to remedy these questions. Both volumes are excellent studies which will be helpful to anyone going through the stages of paring down and understanding their art.
(Ken Harding Amazon Profile)
In my own words
Greetings from a skeptic and book addict! I am a parent, spouse, and professional railroad Conductor with experience in freight and passenger service. I enjoy reading groundbreaking material in the areas of science, sociology, and martial arts. Railroad autobiographies are also fun, 'though few and far between!

Certainly Puts a New Spin on Naifanchi and Sanchin, March 30, 2004
By *Cody* (El Dorado, Ar United States) - *See all my*

reviews

Since most of what I have to say has already been said, but better than I could, I will keep this brief.

If you practice OMA or the JMA derivitives, get this book.

The presentation of the sets and their application is awesome. I practice Isshinryu karate, so of course my sets differ in appearance from these, but it's obvious that the root is the same, and so is the potential for application. Before this book, I was ready to consign my Sanchin practice (sans Ibuki breathing) to a mere upkeep level. But, since I read this text, it is going to be on the front burner of study, along with Naifanchi and Sunsu.

With the exception of the obligatory "crotty history" and certain apparently style-specific techniques on pages 1-79, this book is awesome.

Now, read the other reviews, then buy this book.

Good book for the practicioners of the art., November 15, 1999
By *KYUSHO99*⌄ (United States) - *See all my*
reviews

This book is excellent. It starts off giving the history and origin of Karate which is very interesting. Then it goes right to the point learning. If you want a book that teaches you to relax and also teaches you some self-defence this book is for you. If you learn by reading instructions for the applications of moves it includes that along with detailed pictures. This book is a must have for all martial artists.

Book TWO:
Johnson, N.J. 2000. Barefoot Zen: The Shaolin Roots of Kung Fu and Karate. York Beach, Maine: Samuel Weiser, Inc.

Pat McCarthy Plaudit

"...I was fascinated to experience his [Johnson's] theory and application of Naihanchin... If one was to consider it for what it most likely is, a two-man grappling-hands exercise without worrying about politics, uniform, name etc., then I believe that Nathan's theory would be widely recognised. In fact, I bet that if an Okinawan master had come forward and introduced that which Nathan has already done, he'd probably have been hailed from the highest sources."
Patrick McCarthy. 7th Dan Karate (Butokukai granted Kyoshi grade) Director of International Rykyu Karate Research Group (Plaudit appears on pg 177 and 178 of Barefoot Zen)

General Plaudits
An Improvment on his previous book, Insightful & Enjoyable,
December 29, 2002
By **C. J. Hardman**☑ (San Diego, CA USA) - *See all my reviews*

REAL NAME™

Here Nathan Johnson presents his treatise for the relationship between Buddhist philosophy (primarily zen) and martial arts practice. He considers authenticity in forms, and examines meaning and concepts related to shaolin. I don't fully agree with all of his premises, such as the idea that it is more likely a form is "authentic" when its practitioners credit a Buddhist or Taoist creator (many forms were assigned mysterious origin to make the school or founder credible), has a Buddhist name or title (like Ji-on in shotokan), is simple in its movements, etc. However, Johnson is one of the first who has had the time and energy to research his topics, and formulate theories based upon the how and why, as opposed to simply regurgitating and not questioning older information (the tiresome old "sensei said it, so it is true!" routine).

Johnson also examines karate in the greater context of cultural relativity, pondering such oddities as the esoteric meaning of Sanchin kata ("Sanchin is a mandala..."), and tries his hand (well) at debunking many myths and mistaken notions common in karate and kung fu today. Johnson offers advanced concepts. You don't have to buy all of his theories, but reading this book will definitely encourage you to consider your forms and martial arts in general in a new light.

This second volume is also a great improvement upon the first, as Johnson explains all of the things that I felt were lacking in that book. He relates experiences, correspondences, and includes footnotes and a bibliography of sources, crediting quotes sources. Johnson again demonstrates the fundamental forms of Sanchin and Naihanchin with their applications as in his first book "Zen Shaolin Karate", but the reader has the opportunity to consider his ideas in a wider context. Throughout the time I spent reading this work, I was convinced that this is a highly personal effort, sincere and honest to its heart. Not a grain of arrogance or pretentiousness did I encounter in my reading. Johnson is not trying to force feed us, on the contrary I felt he was encouraging the same spirit of research and discovery among those who consider his words. A worthwhile read for the martial artist who is weary of the mundane and repetitive.

The importance of KATA and how its use at Ryukyu Budo-Kai,
February 15, 2002
By **M. A. Ramos** (Florida USA) - *See all my reviews*

TOP 500 REVIEWER   REAL NAME™   VINE™ VOICE

This book is a must have. It backs up what has been practiced for years at Ryukyu Budo-Kai. This book ties in Zen and Karate, and specifically the KATA. You will see complete examples of Kata and how the bunkai is supposed to be applied. Barefoot Zen also clearly demonstrates that the traditional movements of both Kung Fu and Karate grew from the spiritual practices of the Shaolin order of Buddhist monks and nuns. And follows through to Masters of our time, like Grand Master Nagamine. There is also a section to help you distinguish between what is traditional kata and what has been changed for the modern world. I believe that everything in this book is presented in a straight forward method. This book is a must for all true karateka.
Location:
        Florida USA
Reviewer Rank:
450
See all 832 reviews (9,528 helpful votes)
Listmania! Lists:
7,571 views
See all 5 Listmania! lists (34 helpful votes)
Customer Images:
45*See all 45 customer images*
Nickname:
ihmhermitage

In my own words
I live in Florida, USA. Am interested in Military History and Biblical Studies. I am trying to build an extensive theology library.

I also am doing what I can to rebuild the Immaculate Heart of Mary's Hermitage Chapel and Library located in West Melbourne. Some of the books on my wish list are for the their library.
Interests
Theology, Biblical Studies, History, Monastic Studies.

Zen, Shaolin Fighting System, Creating Lasting Meaning, December 6, 2002

By *Golden Lion "Reader"* ☑ (North Ogden, Ut United States) - *See all my reviews*

TOP 1000 REVIEWER

I really enjoyed this book. The author, Nathan Johnson is an eloquent writer. The book is written in a narrative that provides detailed historical lineages of the most popular martial art disciplines (Kungfu and Okinawan systems) known throughout the world. Most of the book focuses on the principles of zen. Mr Johnson, demonstrates numerous katas and shows how the posture translate into arm twists, throws, and strikes. The application was not design inflict permanent injury rather control. Control rather than injury seems to build his case for the actual interpretation and purpose of the martial art system. He effectively defends his interpretations' of these kata with philosophical discussions about their historical origins, religious Buddhist intent, and zen application. It is clear that Mr Johnson believes that spiritual and moral development is the core belief of the Shaolin Martial Art system teachings. He convinces the reader of this fact by dedicating a chapter to discussing why the Shaolin martial art system was not a system of combat. Mr. Johnson demonstration of pushing hands conveys the message, the Tao is the middle way, "not aggressive and not passive." The hand transformations where used to understand how to blend with resistance or force, neutralize it, and return it to the sender. The book is about the desire of enlightenment, kindness, and hard work and how to achieve lasting meaning in the study of the martial art system.

North Ogden, Ut United States
Reviewer Rank:
668
Nickname:
goldenlionkempo
Web page:
http://www.listensoftware...
In my own words
I'm interest in microtheory pattern matching, learning by questions, feedback, and complex systems.
Interests
Electricity, Physics, Robotics, Nanotechnology, BioTechnology, Biology, Google, History, Visual Studio Dot Net, and Karate

---

Footsteps towards a greater understanding, February 7, 2001

By *David*☑ (Maine ,USA) - *See all my reviews*

This book is an excellent expression of Sensei Johnson's evolution as a man of gung fu. The ideas presented here are of great value in restoring the art and spirit to martial arts. The information is researched diligently, presented honestly, and written clearly. My thanks to the author for the courage of compassion in these days of gladiatorial combat.

Insightful, and illuminating, October 6, 2002

By *Jack W. Mccullough*☑ (Spring Valley, CA USA) – *See all my reviews*

REAL NAME™

Nathan Johnson has done a wonderful job in preparing and presenting the material in this book. His ideas about and research into the truth behind the origins of Kung Fu and Karate kata is unique and insightful. He presents a carefully thought out and well supported argument; that the original kung-fu forms from Shaolin temple were not intended as a combat art. He argues (and I think proves) that forms developed from push hand techniques that were developed for Zen transmission. As a result the (sometimes ridiculous) applications for kata techniques that many of us were taught, are re-examined and more likely applications are presented. I highly recommend this book.

(Jack's) Biography

Jack McCullough is the founding consultant of Razorwire Information Security Consulting. His technical expertise includes wireless and wired networks, computer security, physical security, programming, cryptography, and technical curriculum development. Jacks background includes 10 years of experience in the IT field. He has held positions as IT director, operations manager, network administrator, programmer, and software trainer.

A respected IT and security authority, he is frequently sought out for informational interviews by both broadcast and print media services. Jack has authored books, magazine articles, and white papers on computer security. His written works have been translated into several languages, and many universities have used his books and white papers in information security courses, as have the governments of Australia, the Peoples Republic of China, Japan, Brazil, and Taiwan.

Jack continues to actively research information security, discover new ways to exploit the weaknesses in networked systems, and determine best practices that enable the average computer user to address these threats in an efficient manner. When he isn't writing about or researching technology, Jack teaches karate and self-defense under the watchful eye of Sensei Floyd

---

Burk at the Alpine Karate Academy in Alpine, California, and practices writing about himself in third person.

Editorial Note: My final research concludes that these kata have no 'internal training' or health giving component as Sanchin was originally a weapons kata, and Tensho was created by Miyagi Chojun as late as 1917 (although it could be argued that Miyagi intended a so called 'Internal training' purpose).

Needs work., August 14, 2002
By *M*
 Holmes⌐

The parts of the book dealing with Sanchin and Tensho kata are useful if you have never examined them carefully. The author provides useful interpretations and details for karate students. Regretfully the author omits an entire area of the training in the aforementioned kata, namely internal training, which is the essence of these kata. The author would be well advised to research qi gong training, as would any reader who is determined to study these kata seriously.
Location:
Vancouver, BC, Canada
Reviewer Rank:
Nickname:
bunjinbushi

Book Three:
Johnson, N.J. 2006. The Great Karate Myth: Unravelling the Mysteries of Karate. London: The Wykeham Press.

General Plaudits

Affirmation
I, Nathan J. Johnson affirm and confirm, (to the best of my knowledge) that I do not know, nor have I ever met or communicated directly, or indirectly, with any of the reviewers whose comments follow below, (other than by virtue of the fact that they have read my books). This, of course, excludes Jim Neeter.

★★★★☆ **Interesting & thought provoking, VERY useful. Make sure you get the DVD!**, 5 Dec 2006
By *Terry Tozer "TJSKA.com"* (Reading, UK) - *See all my reviews*

REAL NAME

Another masterpiece from Nathan which will certainly suit both Goju Ryu or Shotokan Styles. It's well written like his other works (e.g.: Zen Shaolin Karate), it's easy to read and made interesting by the use of lots of pictures showing kata like Sanchin & Naihanchin (Tekki for Shotokan readers) and the kata's related application.

He's certainly researched his material very well and gives a nice long historical account of the developments of Naha-te & Shuri-te styles of Okinawan karate which look convincingly accurate.

There are plenty of original Bunkai (kata applications) to get your brain around, all of which Nathan has become famous for, and......all of which stick to the kata's original moves (i.e. there are no extra "made up" bits as in so-called Oyo Bunkai).

The DVD that accompanies the book makes all the difference and is a valuable addition; MAKE SURE YOU GET THE DVD!! I had to write off to the publishers to get my copy.

He interestingly demonstrates SANCHIN kata with the use of Sai on the DVD. In the book he shows many Kung-fu looking wrist breaks (or wrist releases) taken from Sanchin.

It's a pity there aren't more books like this on the market. I'm certain it'll prove to be one of those rare classics one day. Probably suited to the more advanced (Black belt) karate-ka, it is worth every penny.

⭐⭐⭐⭐⭐ **An enquiring mind**, 30 Dec 2006
By **TOHM ECKY** (UK) - *See all my reviews*

This book is essential reading for every person who has a genuine interest in real martial arts instead of a genuine bank balance for magic. If you are scientifically minded and would like martial arts to justify their methods rather than demand faith or suggest that the secrets will come, then this book is for you. If your subject is Kung Fu instead of Karate, you just have to stretch your mind and your reading a little further.

This from Fighting Arts Forum

oneheart Newbie Reged: 08/21/06 Posts: 19	↳**Re: Kodoryu** [Re: *Ed_Morris*] #15895288 - 10/28/06 11:57 AM
	Hey everyone, my names Ryan, I'm a long time lurker, this is my first post. I just finished reading "The Great Karate Myth" and along with Mr. Johnson's other books, thought it was great...not because I agree with all the conclusions he makes, but because he has a unique, well thought out point of view. The "evidence" he gives regarding his theories is mostly, in truth, his opinion, seemingly supported by certain facts, however, how much hard evidence and fact is there regarding kata bunkai? Mr. Johnson presents two main lines of reasoning in support of his theory...the first being physical and the second historical. The physical is by far the most interesting to me and the theory presented goes like this: Karateka have misunderstood kata because kata was, to a large degree, never meant to be practiced without weapons. According to Mr. Johnson, the types of techniques presented and the distances those techniques need to be used at to be effective are the evidence for this line of reasoning. The basic blocking movements and the long punching attacks were all to be performed with sai or tonfa and Bo (or sword?) respectively. The basic katas of the shorin/tomari tradition (minus naihanchi and the "modern katas" created in this century) as well as the three original uechi ryu katas fit in with this category of application. The katas he employs as empty hand katas are Sanchin, Tensho, and Naihanchi, and all of their applications are "touch based" or grappling and practiced using a pushhands format. Now, there are "artifacts" that could be taken as "supporting evidence" for Mr. Johnson's claims from many Chinese and Okinawa systems, such as the Isshinryu use of Kusanku as a sai kata, but I think what is really happening here is that Mr. Johnson is a person who practices both Okinawa karate and wing chun kung fu (as well as being creative and intelligent and I believe buddhist). The above gives him a pretty unique perspective, and I think has caused him

to look for supporting evidence (both physical and historical) of a wing chun type of "structure" to the historical practice of karate kata. This lead him to create a uniquely compact, very systematic approach to applications for Sanchin, tensho and naihanchi as well as an unparalleled reliance upon "contact" and sensitivity in a karate system. I do not think what he presents is the absolute truth regarding kata bunkai, but he has pieced together a truth of his own that is much more coherent than much of what is to be found out there masquerading as karate.The part that really rings true to me is the need for contact based applications. In close quarters, in real confrontations /grappling; kinesthetic sensitivity is the only way to respond to force...the greatest myth in karate practice today is IMHO what we call "sparring". Some of his material, however, is very complicated (some of the tensho grip escapes and the naihanchi material really fights me) and while it may have a function in the pushands format used by kodo ryu, has little value from a self defense stand point (Mr. Johnson does however point out that his is not nessicarily a self defense system)

('Oneheart' [Ryan] 2006)

And:

oneheart Newbie	⌐Re: Kodoryu [Re: *student_of_life*] #15895534 - 10/29/06 03:48 PM	
Reged: 08/21/06 Posts: 19	...I challenge anyone to "prove" conclusively what any pre 1950's kata is for. I believe that Mr. Johnson has presented a very interesting perspective. I don't accept them as gospel, just say that they are interesting and provide substantial food for thought. Many people today have "created their own system," and Mr. Johnson is no different save one thing. He has created something that is to a large degree, internally consistent. This is my interest in his work. We can argue about what "proof" means all day, but that is not very interesting (not to me at least...) I would love to address this topic in more detail, but my time today is limited.	

('Oneheart' [Ryan] 2006)

Finally:

shoshinkan [M] needs no title Reged: 05/10/05 Posts: 2499 Loc: UK	**Re: Kodoryu** [Re: *butterfly*] #15894700 - 10/26/06 01:18 PM Hi Butterfly, LOL, yes I guess my point of view is an odd one. OK I shall be clear this time, I got alot out of Barefoot Zen, a mixture of Nathan's Sensei point of view and hard fact was most interesting to me. The Great Karate myth is IMO one of the best researched books around, reading through it I found very interesting for the same reasons as above. However the conclusions I disagree with but the works themselves are superb. Having met and trained with Ko-Do ryu people I found their karate to be very good indeed so I guess im supporting their efforts perhaps more than I normally would. A few years back I found the rather strange ability to get along with people and accept them even when I think along different lines! I guess it's called an open mind. -------------------- Jim Neeter *www.shoshinkanuk.blogspot.com*

(Neeter 2006)

The following (partial) review is taken from
http://www.karatedo-forum.com

I cannot properly identify the author as I am not a member, however...

WombatO neSix	☐Aug 2 2006, 02:56 AM Post #1
Sifu Group: Admin. Posts: 1924 Joined: 5- February 04 From: Walsall. Member No.: 144 Style: Yang style Tai- Chi+Kobud o	BOOK REVIEW THE GREAT KARATE MYTH by NATHAN JOHNSON ...But this book really is just more than one mans idea of what karate is, its a history of far eastern Martial-Arts in general, its a debunking of the so-called "secret techniques" found in karate, which prove - more often than not - to be no more then thought and hard work. For instance, the deadly Dim Mak or "death touch" - if a western boxer expires after a match, no one puts it down to a mystical blow - its more likely to be internal bleeding or head trauma. But the really surprising thing about this book is how its written. It's easy on the eye, a joy to read, and even a complete thicko like myself managed to understand alot of his theories and ideas. I'll be honest with you now, the book is fairly pricey (as are most good Martial-Arts books), but considering what you get - and what you learn from it - the price justifies itself completely. Having read it from cover to cover, I would have happily paid more for it (And given the circumstances of how I bought the book, probably double) I don't think anyone can profess to know everything about karate, but if just one person can read this book and go away with a whole new point of view - as I did, then it complements their training as a whole. I know i'll never look at Tensho in the same way again! Read it. You won't regret it.

See also SENI, Europe's most prestigious Martial Arts convention.

http://www.kodoryu.com/pdf/SeniShowFlyer.pdf

Recommended Reading for Karate Kata Researchers

Shuri-te kata

Excellent examples of original Shuri-te kata were recorded by Nagamine Shoshin in his *Okinawan Karate-do: The Preservation of a Legacy,* Tokyo: (Shinjinbutsuorai-sha 1975). This seminal work, translated By K. Shinzato and M. Shiroma, was re-titled and published by Charles E. Tuttle in 1976 as *The Essence of Okinawan Karate-Do.* It has had some twenty printings! Long association (read perseverance) with this work (particularly the Naihanchin kata) led to what I consider to be the original (grappling) purpose of that kata Naihanchin and to understanding Kusanku. The kata are well preserved in this remarkable volume.

Naha-te kata

In contrast to the 'shifting sands' of Shuri-te kata, which have changed considerably in the Shotokan and Wado Ryu formats, and unlike the kata of Goju Ryu (the bulk of which, I suggest in *The Great Karate Myth* are post-modern) the Uechi kata remain virtually unchanged. George Mattson, a respected Uechi Ryu Karate Sensei of many years standing, recorded two of the three 'core' Naha kata in *The Way of Karate,* Rutland Vermont, Tokyo: Tuttle 1963. These two kata provide enough information to grasp the essence of Naha kata.

The *kata* presented in these two books, both of which I acquired in August 1979, have influenced me greatly. *I highly recommend them to all Karate and Kung Fu researchers.*

References

Abernathy, I., ed., no date. A Brief History of Kata. *Yoshukai Karate International* [online]. *http://www.yoshukaikarateinternational.com/Kata_History_2.html* [Accessed 22Aug 2008].

Ashihara Karate International. *Why the Need for Basics?* [online]. Technique page: Ashihara Karate International. Available from: *http://www.ashiharakarate.org/html/technique.html* [Accessed 17 August 2008].

Block, Jenny., 2008. *'Flamers and Lurkers and Trolls, Oh My'* [online]. Available at: http://www.huffingtonpost.com/jenny-block/flamers-and-lurkers and-t_b_115614.html [Accessed 20 August 2008].

Funakoshi, G., 2001. (1925) *Karate Jutsu: formerly Rentan Goshin Karate Jutsu*: translated byJohn Teramoto. Tokyo: Kodansha International

Hisatomi, T., 1898. *Hayanawa Kappo Kenpo Kyohan Zukai Zen* [online] Tokyo, Kiseido. Available from: *http://museum.hikari.us/books/kenpo/index.html* [Accessed 25 August 2008].

Johnson, N J., 2000. *Barefoot Zen*: *The Shaolin Roots of Kung Fu and Karate*. Weiser: York Beach Maine.

King, G., 24 July 2006. Shikon. com. [online]. Link deleted. (Archived 24 July 2006.) *http://www.shikon.com/forum/viewtopic.php?t=1926&postdays=0&postorder=ach&h.* [Accessed 24 July 2006].

King, G., 25 Oct 2006. Re: Kodryu. Fighting Arts.com. [online]. Available from: *http://www.fightingarts.com/ubbthreads/showflat.php?Cat=0&Number=15894288&page=0&fpart=2&vc=1* [Accessed 8 August 2008].

Lee, B., 1975. *The Tao of Jeet Kune Do*. U.S. Ohara Inc.
Mattson, G., 1963. *The WayofKarate*. RutlandVermont: Tokyo, Tuttle.

McCarthy, P and McCarthy Y., 2002. *Motobu Choki: Karate, MyArt.* International Ryukyu Karate Research Group.

McCarthy, P., 1995. Private letter, *In*: N.J.Johnson, *Barefoot Zen: The Shaolin Roots of Kung Fu and Karate.* York Beach Maine: Weiser, pp.177-178.

Mike, Sensei., 16 Sept 2002. Japanese Martial Arts Talk. [online]. Available from: http://www.martialtalk.com/forum/showthread.php?t=3754 [Accessed 23 July 2008]

Morris, Ed., 25 Oct 2006. Re Kodoryu. Fighting Arts.com. [online]. Available from: *http://www.fightingarts.com/ubbthreads/showflat.php?Cat=0&Number=15894288&page=0&fpart=2&vc=1* [Accessed 08 Aug. 2008]

Neeter, Jim., 26 Oct. 2006. Re: Kodryu. Fighting Arts.com [online]. Available from: *http://www.fightingarts.com/ubbthreads/showflat.php?Cat=0&Number=15894288&page=0&fpart=2&vc=1* [Accessed 14 Aug 2008].

Noble, G., 1995. The First Karate Books: Part One. *Fighting Arts International,* (number 90), pp. 19 – 23.

Oneheart., 28 Oct 2006. Re: Kodoryu. Fighting Arts.com [online]. Available from: *http://www.fightingarts.com/ubbthreads/showflat.php?Cat=0&Number=15894288&page=0&fpart=2&vc=1* [Accessed 14 Aug 2008]

Oneheart., 29 Oct. 2006. Re: Kodryu. Fighting Arts.com. [online]. Available from: *http://www.fightingarts.com/ubbthreads/showflat.php?Cat=0&Number=15894288&page=0&fpart=2&vc=1* [Accessed 14 Aug. 2008]

Pressimone, Tommy., 10 June 2008. *Practice Kata Until the Techniques Become Second Nature?* [online]. Available from: *http://tommypkarate.blogspot.com/2008/03/putting-things-in-perspective.html* [Accessed 14 Aug 2008]

Redmdond, Rob., 27 Dec 2007. *The Rise of Kata Application.* [online]. Available from: *http://www.24fightingchickens.com/2007/12/27/the-rise-of-kata-application/>* [Accessed 10 Aug. 2008]

Rowe, Steve., 31 Oct 2006. Re: Kodoryu. Fighting Arts.com. [online]. Available from: http://www.fightingarts.com/ubbthreads/showflat.php?Cat=0&Number=15894288&page=0&fpart=8&vc=1 [Accessed 9 Aug 2008].

Stone, Matt., 16 Sept 2002. Japanese Martial Arts Talk. Available from: *http://www.martialtalk.com/forum/showthread.php?t=3754* [Accessed 11 Aug 2008].

'Student of Life'., 26 Oct 2006. Re: Kodoryu. Fighting Arts.com. [online post]. Available from: *http://www.fightingarts.com/ubbthreads/showflat.php?Cat=0&Number=15894288&page=0&fpart=2&vc=1* [Accessed 06 Aug. 2008].

Wikipedia. Swan., no date. [online] Available from: *http://en.wikipedia.org/wiki/Swan*) [Aaccessed 2 Aug 2008]

www.ingramcontent.com/pod-product-compliance
Lightning Source LLC
Chambersburg PA
CBHW060632280326
41933CB00012B/2012